CONTINUITY OF LIFE · VOLUME 1

Endings Are Beginnings

Navigating Your Hard Times into Higher States

Written and Illustrated by Dr. Angela deAngelis

Continuity of Life Series

Volume 1

Endings Are Beginnings:

Navigating Your Hard Times into Higher States

Volume 2

Embracing Eternity:

The Life Force Does Not Die

Volume 3

Transition and Survival Technologies:

Interdimensional Consciousness as Healing, Survival and Beyond

Volume 4

Healing Earth in All Her Dimensions:

Personal, Species and Planetary Healing Tools

Endings Are Beginnings

Navigating Your Hard Times into Higher States

Written and Illustrated by
Dr. Angela deAngelis

Light Technology Publishing

ISBN 1-891824-62-7
EAN 978-1-891824-62-3

Published & Printed by

Light Technology Publishing
www.lighttechnology.com

800-450-0985

PO Box 3540
Flagstaff, AZ 86003
publishing@lighttechnology.net

Contents

List of Figures

Author's Note

Thank you for visiting these pages. Our paths will touch awhile as this little book becomes a doorway into life, into one another and into ourselves. We will share some hours, some ideas and some feelings on these joined but separate journeys we call our lives. Here there are no barriers, no beginnings and no endings. Here the continuity of life grabs hold, makes its reality loud and clear. Here the life force makes its ongoing, ever-present essence known. Here metaphors for truth and reality are presented for readers to take in as they wish—via their imaginations, their intellects or their souls, or in all or other ways at once. In fact, calling this psychologically, theologically and spiritually based material an "instructional metaphor," or even science-fiction or fantasy, may be the best way for some readers to choose to read it, and this is perfectly, wonderfully fine.

This book, *Endings Are Beginnings: Navigating Your Hard Times into Higher States*, is Volume One of the four-volume *Continuity of Life* series. This first volume forms a basic foundation for the more detailed and advanced volumes that follow it. Herein lies information that will help you to begin seeing life as cyclic rather than linear, to begin seeing endings (and deaths) as anything but absolute endings. Rather, endings are natural phases of cycles that continuously begin and end, and begin and end, and begin and end, and begin again and again. Truly "begin" and "end" are merely words for ever-streaming processes. These are transitions that we may not be able to gain a larger view of as we undergo them. Sometimes the minor or major confusion or intensity of a transition distracts us from the fact that it is a transition. We may feel too unsettled or maybe even too frightened to map the process. Sometimes transitions feel like struggles or very hard times, like deaths we cannot survive. But we *can* navigate these hard times into higher states. These hard times can be experienced differently if we allow ourselves to see the larger picture. In fact, all transitions can be steps into new levels of being. Transitions happen. Why not make them as worthwhile as we can?

This book begins to describe and map transition and death, setting the stage for the more advanced mappings and techniques presented in the following volumes. This book begins with basic understandings of cycles and a rethinking of endings. Rethinking the process of death—whether it be the death of a phase of life, of a behavior, of a relationship or the death of a body—and making the most out of every transition are the messages here. The following volumes take this thinking deeper, presenting techniques and tools for surviving transitions, endings and deaths, and for participating in the wondrous continuity of life. This knowledge is our birthright, and it is for us to use, to understand, to maximize and to carry with us into the next level of our existence as we survive.

No particular belief system is required of readers here. The consciousness technologies herein are available to everyone regardless of religion or non-religion. Readers who do practice a particular religion will find that this material neither denies nor threatens that religion. You see, this book is about the further evolution of the human consciousness.

The Never-Ending Stream

By what amazing grace
have we arrived here,
lost and found,
ending and beginning,
again.

The thread, the spirit of life,
weaves on and on
as we intertwine
with all around us
and all within
and all eternity.

A never-ending stream of
all things we were,
we are, and
we will be . . .

— Angela deAngelis

EMBRACE
revolution brought by conscious death

RIDE
personal apocalypse into power

HARVEST
death

SHED
skin

MASTER
transition from one reality to another

MAP
deaths

MOVE
death into transcendence

ALLOW
patterning to die

SEE
physical death as a model

OVERCOME
apocalypse syndrome

KNOW
life's cyclic nature

NAVIGATE YOUR HARD TIMES INTO HIGHER STATES!

BASIC LIGHT-ENERGY-ACTION-PROCESS STEPS

LEAP Level	LEAP Type	Volume of *Continuity of Life* Series This Is Discussed In
Seeing Cycles	Ground Level of LEAPs	Volume One
One	Embracing	Volume Two
Two	Quickening	Volume Two
Three	Willing the Exit	Volume Two
Four	Leaping to the Next Dimension	Volume Three
Five	Ascending	Volume Three
Six	Catharting Beyond	Volume Three
Seven	Metascending to a New Niche	Volume Four
Eight	Achieving Metastasis and High Metaxis	Volume Four

Preface: Come Fly with the Phoenix

It is never, ever too late, even when the path looks too difficult to survive. You may find yourself struggling in the rubble of broken dreams. You may have been there a moment, a month or a decade. You may feel pain, tears, a sense of loss or hopelessness. You may just feel confusion. Or you may feel nothing at all. You may say, "Please, please someone fix this. Please, please show me a way out. Please, please, higher power or God, if you are out there, help me."

You may find the bits and pieces of the life you wanted to lead scattered around you, shattered. You may weep or you may scream or you may sit in numb silence. You tread carefully through the fragments of your fractured dreams because you hurt when you walk on them, as if they are broken glass and your feet are bare.

Everywhere you look, you think you see a wasteland, your own personal wasteland. But these bits are the ingredients of something new. Put them together, like pieces of a jigsaw puzzle, and you will solve the mystery of the new you. There is a secret among these ruins, something new waiting for you to see it. There is always time to begin again . . . always!

And then a hand reaches out from somewhere, a hand you can almost see. Is it your imagination, or is someone really there? Look again: The hand you see is your own. Yes, there may be others trying to help, or you may feel all alone in this, but the hand you see is your own. You are calling yourself into the continuity of life. Listen. You want to be heard. You want to come back.

The view from this rock-bottom place is the best view ever. Open your eyes. From here you can truly see. The possibilities are endless. Believe that you can resurrect yourself—believe!—and you will. This is a phase of a long and continuing cycle, not an ending, but a beginning.

Chapter 1

Know Life's Cyclic Nature

This chapter frames all endings we undergo as parts of larger cycles: endings with new beginnings. When we see everything that takes place as cyclic, concern about and fear of change and endings can shift to a more constructive focus.

This book is written for anyone who is undergoing, has undergone or will undergo a major ending or transition, or a death of any sort—which, of course, is everyone. This includes divorce, being fired, leaving home or having one's children leave home. It includes abrupt changes or endings, such as having one's home collapse in an earthquake, receiving a serious injury or having something precious stolen. It also includes gradual but definite changes, such as changes in behavioral patterns—shifting out of a steady or addictive relationship to a drug, a person or a behavior; outgrowing a stage of life, a philosophy, a religion or a cult; aging or having all one's oldest friends die; or undergoing the disease process, whether it is temporary, chronic or "terminal." And, of course, we include the concept of dying, with which we all think we are so familiar:

physical death, which is seen by many people as the ultimate form of death. Indeed, physical death—fear of it, avoidance of it, viewing it as final—is an excellent model for all the deaths, small and large, that each and every one of us endures.

You Can Make It Through

The word "endure" is used here because all deaths and all endings can be endured. You can make it through any ordeal, no matter how impossible "making it through" seems to be, no matter how impossible the transition appears to be. On some level, you already know this. You have already been through many profound transitions in your lifetime. You have been born, you have walked your first steps, you may have been breastfed and then weaned. You likely had a first day of school, had a favorite pet die, became an adolescent, fell in love for the first time, had sex for the first time, broke up with your first boyfriend or girlfriend, finished school and left home. You've probably gotten a job (or several jobs), been laid off or fired, been married and/or divorced, or have experienced some other life change. You have probably mourned the death of a family member or friend.

Of course, not all of these are considered entirely sorrowful, unpleasant or difficult experiences. Why, then, do many of these endings, these experiences, feel at least a little bit like death? Because all changes—all transitions or endings of phases, whether they seem to be good or bad—are types of death. We must allow ourselves to stretch the meaning of the word death in this way in order to fully understand and appreciate cycles of life. Certainly we feel changes and transitions. Frequently these are growing pains. Sometimes this is the pain of not growing when we need to.

Any ending or death can be somewhat unsettling, as are many

transitional experiences. Endings can be disturbing, frightening and even painful when we cannot see them as otherwise. However, we can learn how to see and experience what we think of as "painful" experiences as something else and to use these experiences well. Look back on your life. Think of the many experiences you found to be difficult or painful as they were happening, that you later saw as not so bad or useful, maybe even as great motivators, instructors or sources of inspiration.

Death Is Birth, and There May Be Labor Pains

Pain is more than just a four-letter word. Pain is a sensation that seems to hurt. Anyone who has experienced intense pain knows that the sensation of pain is real—about as real as any experience we ever encounter. Pain cannot be denied. However, pain itself can be understood differently; it can be reframed to help move the painful sensations into higher states.

Those readers who have given birth to babies may know the feeling of labor pains—pain that cycles in and out, traveling through layers or rings of pain that quicken over time until the baby is born. Think of any ending or death process, including physical death, as giving birth to yourself and the emotional and physical pain as labor pain. Now there is a direction to the pain and an outcome to the process. This outcome is a birth into a new reality: your new reality. Again, death, the death of anything—your marriage, your way of life, your body—is merely a transition, a passage. It would be dishonest to say that death is not an ending. It *is* an ending, and it is a transition into a new beginning. Again, all endings are beginnings.

Not all endings are painful or traumatic. Every day begins and ends, cycling through day and night. Every breath you take

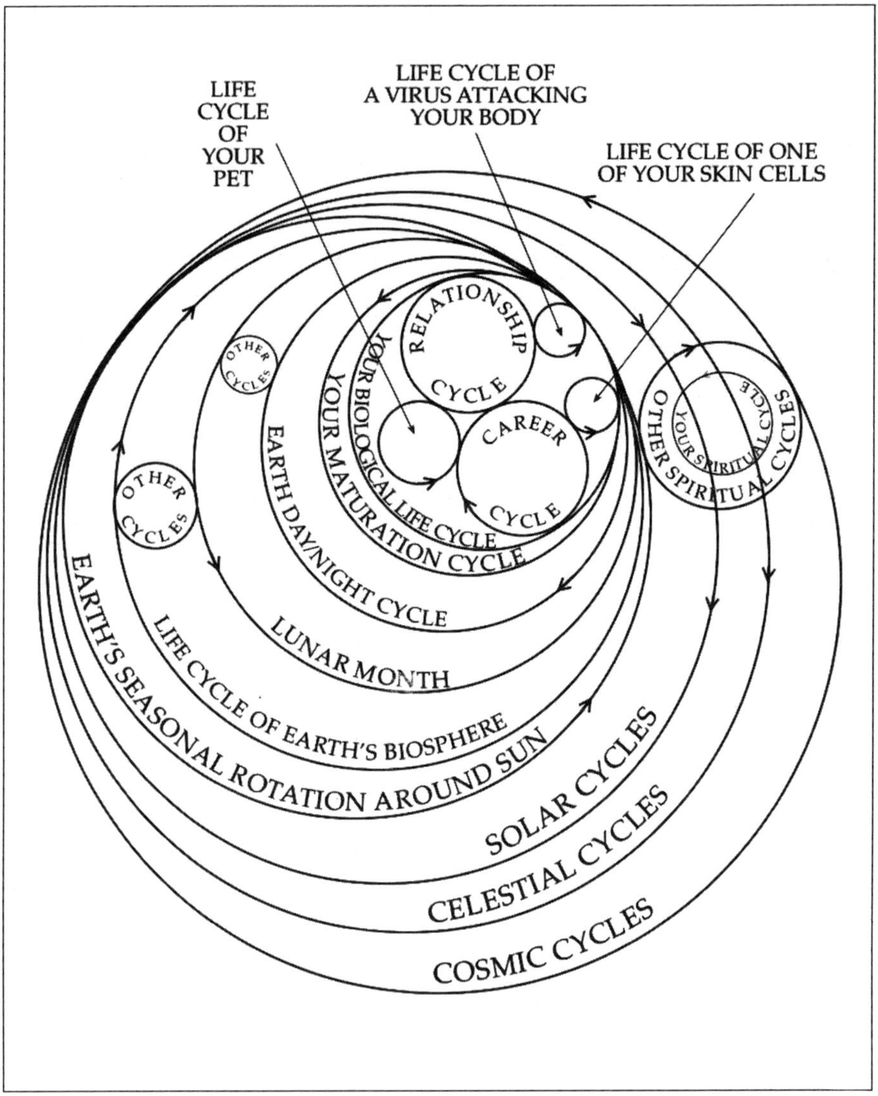

Figure 1.1. Life's cyclical nature among encompassing cycles.

begins and ends, cycling through an inhale/exhale process. Everything you do has a cycle to it. We tend to move right through many endings and beginnings, too busy to realize that we have just survived one of the infinite number of transitions we undergo every single day. We also tend to pay little attention to the many other, far larger cycles we are living within and around. Figure 1.1 depicts this reality—that we live in and around cycles within cycles within cycles within cycles within cycles.

You Can Navigate Transition

We may not feel we have time to consciously navigate every single transition we undergo every single minute of our lives. However, we can incorporate increased consciousness into any activity we want to be more aware of. Conscious behavior is possible on all fronts—for example, conscious breathing, conscious eating, conscious relating and conscious spending.

Do you recall the old adage, "Use it or lose it"? Indeed, even the power of consciousness can and must be exercised to maximize its abilities. Awareness is like a muscle, and it can be strengthened with exercise. Practicing being more conscious helps strengthen the consciousness to prepare it for times when being more conscious can help navigate a challenging experience or transition. Basically, with this practice, we are training our cognitive mental functions to enhance their metacognitive levels.

Awakening the Metacognition

Metacognition is not as difficult as it may sound. In fact, we are using our metacognitive processes all the time. In this sense, we are already quite adept at metacognition. Our minds process information and information about that information on a continuous basis. For the most part, we are unaware of the constant work we are doing to process stimuli. We just see, hear, taste, smell and touch, without thinking about the massive amount of electro-biochemical translations being made every single millisecond. Compounding the massive amount of information processing that our biological brains and nervous systems are doing at all times is the equally enormous amount of responsive processing involved in our responses to the information we process and perceive. This includes our responses to our responsive responses, and our responses to these responses, and so on.

Our brains set up higher mental functions to manage, identify, organize, retain and respond to the constant stream of incoming and interactively incoming stimulation we are constantly receiving. This super or supra level of information processing we do is the metacognition referred to above, which functions virtually invisibly—unless we call our own attention to our own metacognitive processes. So, meet your metacognition! Say hello to your higher cognitive functions. Own your metacognition, wake it up, train it and help it help you to go conscious, to go very conscious. This will not only make all your transitions and deaths much easier, it will make all the processes that you are constantly undergoing far richer.

When we face a challenging or painful transition, conscious and metacognitive navigation is an immense plus. It is how you navigate a transition that will set the stage for your next beginning. The more you understand this process—the great adventure of ending and death—the more you can use the experience to consciously, with your full attention at work, create the next phase of your life and design your new reality.

Death, in any form, is indeed a great adventure. It is a challenging, wondrous, remarkable journey every time you take it. No two deaths are the same; however, the passage we call death has characteristics that can be identified again and again. Learning to consciously recognize these characteristics, these landmarks along the road of transition, will ease your passage, enhance the richness of your experience, ensure your survival (in whatever form your consciousness wishes to survive) and determine the quality of that survival (the richness of the harvest) you take from your death.

You Can Harvest Pain and Transition for Initiation

You can harvest your transitions and deaths. Your harvest can be as abundant as you wish it to be. You can learn as much as you want from anything you undergo. You can harvest a strengthened, fortified, quickened self from the process of transition. Even if the transition is one of the more challenging passages you undergo during your life (a troubled divorce or other family breakup; a major downturn in financial, career, health or social status; a physical disaster of some sort; or physical death itself), you can transform the process. You can transform your experience of the process—transform it from merely a tough or miserable ordeal, merely a disaster through which you seem to be aimlessly and hopelessly tumbling, into a profound initiation. You can transform yourself in the process.

Again, this is not to deny any pain that may be experienced. We all know pain, some of us more directly and intensely than others. Pain cannot be denied, and it is unfair to deny the reality of another's pain simply because we are not feeling it. Pain is present in many intense experiences. Given that pain is present, why not put the experience of pain to work? Why not allow the pain to be useful in deepening the self, the awareness, the knowledge and the soul of the person experiencing the pain (either directly or indirectly by witnessing or sensing it)?

Pain does far more than just hurt. Both emotional and physical pain call our attention to the fact that something is taking place. Pain can be a sign of change or of the need for change. While change can seem to hurt, so can not changing when change is needed. We may be stuck and need to move through a situation—go into transit mode—or we may be moving through the situation and registering the experience as painful. When we are stuck, we may need to resolve the pressure or relieve the stuck sensation by consciously entering into or moving deeper into a transition process.

Whether it be emotional or physical pain, pain can be part of or can be transformed into something that is a part of an initiation process. Initiation? Yes, initiation—into the next phase, a new way of seeing the world, a new self. A lot of energy is contained in pain. Therefore, pain can be fuel for change, when pain is understood in this way. Pain can be harvested for growth, survival and transcendence. In this sense, even a painful physical death is a great initiation. On some level, we are aware of this. Yet few people consciously prepare for this initiation-by-death, or any of their other seemingly smaller initiation-by-living-death adventures. This is because we tend to avoid or even be afraid of great emotional or physical pain. But this means that we also avoid great changes, great risks and great unknowns. So we do not consciously plan for changes and transitions, except to buy insurance, write wills and pray for some kind of salvation or direction.

Obstacles to Surviving Transition Well

However, it is not only fear that keeps us from preparing for initiation-by-death. Fear is one of four states of mind that keep us from knowing how to plan for, manage, take control of, successfully endure and harvest our dying processes. Next to fear is our deep programming, the behavioral and energetic patterning that we are programmed to be addicted to. And next to pattern addiction is lack of information: we have not been taught the true nature of death. We have either denied ourselves or have been denied the truth about our existence. And beyond these states of mind is the social state of mind: the cultural taboos and laws we have developed and enacted against learning how to die well, and even against actually dying a physical death with grace. [See Figure 1.2.]

1) Fear
2) Deep programming
3) Lack of information
4) Cultural taboos and laws

Figure 1.2. The four states of mind that are obstacles to surviving transition well.

This is definitely not to advocate suicide as an impulsive, desperate way out of the challenges of life. In fact, many suicides are committed in order to avoid the challenges of life rather than to engage in or grow from them. Rarely is suicide a consciously spiritually navigated event. When it is, then the individual is making clear choices and is fully conscious of the impact of this event upon the self and others. Various religions have various views on suicide and it is up to each reader to choose her or his own approach to suicide.

This book does not take a position on either suicide or euthanasia. This book does, however, advocate in favor of an adult individual's right to choose her or his own view on these matters, and the human right to decide how and when to be involved in the process of death. Even the ability to leave the physical body at will without having to "commit suicide" is present within us. Numerous ancient cultures' teachings (as well as some modern-day practices found primarily among people practicing ancient traditions) feature this form of self-willed, consciously selected body departure. Each person has the inalienable right to choose for himself what sort of death to have—where, when and how—so long as that person is making a responsible choice. The matter of responsible choice will be discussed later.

You Can Determine How You Travel through Transition

You can decide for yourself how much emotional and physical suffering you undergo in any of your deaths, physical or otherwise. Why do most of us not know this? Consider the possibility that we have been denied the truth about death—by religions, by political leaders, by those among us who know. Why deny us truth? Because we as individuals and as whole populations are likely to be much easier to control if we spend our energy worrying about, avoiding or denying death. We are much easier to control through our fears, our pattern addictions, our lack of information and our explicit and implicit cultural, religious and legislative taboos against knowing.

Were each and every one of us able to ride personal, social and global disaster; personal, social and global apocalypse; personal, social and global death into greater consciousness and power, we would be an entirely different people. We would be more powerful as individuals and as a collective life force. Whatever forces from within us or outside us are attempting to hold us captive, they will be severely threatened when we become masters of our own death. In other words, the fears and limitations we feel and have grown to believe are actual may simply be part of the brainwashing we have endured for so long. We are not prisoners of false limitations once we have the key to exit the land of narrow beliefs. And we have that key.

Master Endings, Master Beginnings

I am inviting you to become exactly this: a captain of your own endings, a master of your own deaths. This will enable you to master your life. After all, we are always living and dying, and so is our world. Rethink the concept of death for yourself and for all humanity. Our survival, our freedom of will, depends upon the spreading of this awareness.

You will grow to understand this on a deep level as you explore what you find in this book and as the awareness of this material revives in your soul. These latent ideas about the death process will flow into your conscious and metacognitive intelligence gently and will allow you to take them as lightly or profoundly as you wish—as you feel ready for. These ideas will actually identify, refine and clarify themselves as you grow more conscious of them; they will be flowing to and from the population and your own unconscious and subconscious, to and from our collective consciousness and into your consciousness. [see Figure 1.3]. You wake up, someone else wakes up, the next person wakes up, the population wakes up. This book, and you, will fuel this process, awakening the essential key understandings of transition, change and death that we all carry.

collective unconscious

↕

individual unconscious ↔ individual subconscious

↕

individual consciousness

↕

collective consciousness

Figure 1.3. The path of consciousness.

Thank you for joining in understanding in a deep way that endings are beginnings, and knowing this for yourself, for those around you, for humanity and for this planet we call Earth. This journey is yours, so make it your own! Master the ride of your life. This is what the journey of life is all about—seeing the process.

Meet endings, meet all kinds of deaths and know life on all levels. We have a right to know these things on all levels. We have a right to rethink what our lives are about, to reassess the meaning of everything we do, have done and will do. The suppression of knowledge key to the survival of your consciousness, to the survival of all of us, must end. The time has come for the removal of our ignorance.

Chapter 2

Overcome: The Apocalypse Syndrome

This chapter views fear of change, calamity and death as driving forces that tend to block the ability to see what is actually taking place and truly explore the opportunities being presented.

Now we are ready to unmask death and see its face. The mask itself is surprisingly easy to remove. Yet behind the mask are many layers of faces. Close to the surface is the crust of fear.

Distinguishing between Fears

Fear affects much of what goes on within and around us. So much fear is subconscious that we may even miss recognizing that it is present and driving us. Let's examine this fear, look it in the eye. Have you ever been afraid? Have you ever examined your fear? Was it a help or a hindrance to you? To master death, whatever the sort of death or transition being faced, we must see the difference between two basic types of fear: fear as help, and fear as a hindrance to survival.

When used well, fear serves a purpose. However, when used well, what we call "fear" is better described as "protective awareness." For example, being afraid of an auto accident does less to prevent an accident than being very alert and highly aware of the other vehicles, people and animals on the road. Paying attention is a very good idea. Being so scared that you cannot protect yourself is not a good idea. When fear clouds the consciousness, it is not being used well; it is blinding fear.

This distinction is especially critical on the population or social level. Not everyone who warns of physical, environmental, political, economic or other dangers or disasters is sick with blinding fear. Some of these persons are calling important developments to our attention, suggesting that in order to have a conscious say in or conscious response to the course of events, we pay attention and maybe even take action. Too often, those who seek to alert us to things, events or forces that may affect us undesirably and overtake us against our will are criticized or labeled as "paranoid" or "overly fearful" or "wrong" or even "crazy." This is unfortunate, as protective awareness is of great value. A respectable futurist or prophet is often taken far too lightly. Still, discerning the difference between flat-out fantasy and sound warning is key.

flat-out fantasy ← versus → sound warning

But do we have this key in our possession? Knowing the difference is indeed a challenge. We think of sirens as helpful (even essential!) warning sounds coming from fire engines, police cars and air-raid warnings. We trust that these sirens are sounded to protect us in some way. However, do we carry with us a deep distrust of warnings, knowing that not all warnings are accurate or even protective? Think all the way back to the story of the siren in ancient mythology, where the term "siren song" referred to an appeal or cry that was hard to resist, even seductive, but if heeded would lead to a bad result. Messages, invitations and even warnings can indeed be seductive. They carry a momentum and magnetism of their own. Therefore, we must keep ourselves clear enough emotionally to discern the difference between a seductive false warning and a too-often-ignored valid one. Fear can muddle our ability to recognize the difference.

false warning ← versus → valid warning

Certainly there is a problem with knowing what to believe. Can we tell the difference between useful information coming out of protective awareness and the stasis and chaos that come from the projection of blinding fear? We humans have lived with so many fear-inducing lies for so long that we confuse these with valid warnings of impending danger. It becomes frighteningly difficult to tell the difference. We will return to this concept when we talk about the fear of death and about the misinformation and disinformation about death that may be generating these fears.

Defining Apocalypse Syndrome

Why are we so frequently unable to clearly sense this difference between protective awareness and blinding fear? This is likely because we have been genetically, culturally and spiritually programmed to carry within us a condition, a disease, that we can best call the apocalypse syndrome. The apocalypse syndrome afflicts many who feel a sort of impending doom. This syndrome clouds the discernment process and makes it difficult to know whether a fear is one we must listen to for our own and others' safety, or a free-floating anxiety that is attaching itself to the nearest possible or even impossible problem or threat. Confusion and fear mix together into a blurry cocktail of unknowns that tend to at least emotionally paralyze those who drink it.

projection of blinding fear ← versus → protective awareness

This condition or syndrome is riddled with real and imagined sensations (and questions about these sensations) that confuse the mind. What is the difference between a real and an imagined sensation, between a real and an imagined fear? Is there one? Does it matter whether a sensation is reality-based or not? After all, what is reality? What is a valid concern and what is not? How do we know? If kept to a dull roar and considered calmly, these can be very good questions. Using them as part of a process of learning to discern for oneself what the choices are, what beliefs can be accepted or discarded, is part of the awakening of the metacognition. Coming up with personal ways of knowing what is true for oneself, without outside influence dictating this, is key.

Traditional Apocalypse

Take some time to think about the meaning of the word "apocalypse" and what your conscious mind does with this concept. Whether or not your subconscious mind pays any attention to this concept is less important for the moment. The term "apocalypse" comes from the Greek word *apokalypsis*, meaning "disclosure." Apocalypse was originally defined as some kind of major, all-involving disaster in which forces of good and evil would clash and from which, in the end, only supernatural intervention could preserve good.

According to most definitions of apocalypse, communication with divine forces should disclose or reveal the timing, force and characteristics of an apocalypse. Many religions therefore include "divine revelation." Some of these revelations are said to come to humans directly from a God; however, apparently, in said reality, only a few humans can read them. Many other revelations are said to come from a God but through designated go-betweens or intermediaries who may be shamans, religious leaders or persons with special abilities or special status.

Most major religions include references to one or more apocalyptic or cataclysmic events. These are often said to take place at the end of a cycle of time. At the end of such a cycle, piety is said to be dead; fire, drought and famine to ravage the Earth; and a century (or a long spell) of death to follow. According to several apocalypse stories, despite flooding, all the moisture on and in the Earth will begin to dry up. Eventually, a universal conflagration of some sort will eliminate the last human occupants, and all the Earth will be consumed in a vast whirlpool of flame. There is usually a supernatural way for "believers" and "the chosen ones" to survive.

This is common apocalypse teaching carried by many of the world's great religions. It is also most likely carried deep within our cellular or genetic memories, as depictions of this process do appear again and again in human religion and mythology. Many of these myths include the same ingredients: increasing tribulation; the moral dissolution of humankind; the emergence of some kind of major war; the fracturing and collapse of the Earth's crust; and, later, the sinking of landmasses, even entire continents, into the sea. The atmosphere becomes darkened, stars (including comets and meteors and maybe even moons) crash down to Earth from the sky, and a massive fire of some sort fills much of the atmosphere. Of course, this end is also a beginning, as new yugas or time cycles begin after major apocalypses, with the same cycles appearing repeatedly. Eventually, the same ultimate fate evolves. Again and again from the ashes of the cosmic fire arises the phoenix, the flight of life born anew. Even this ultimate ending is a beginning!

This quick overview is not to minimize the reality of apocalypse. Modern science tells us that the Earth has surely witnessed comet impacts and massive disasters of global or near global proportions that killed off entire groups of species—the dinosaurs, for example. And such disasters can happen again; they may be part of our larger cosmic destiny. There is more to history on Earth than we teach ourselves.

Much of the truth about Earth's history has been lost. However, the collective memory has managed to keep some form of this information alive for us all, preserving it not only in mythical and religious form throughout history, but also in symbolic imagery deeply imbedded in that collective memory or mind—perhaps even encoded into the genetics that grow that mind. Here we must pause to wonder, if images of apocalypse are indeed coded into our collective memories, how did those images get there, and are they placed there to protect us or to scare us into being more easily controlled? Are these images manipulated by those who understand the power to be had in using others' fears and fear mechanisms?

Personal Apocalypse

Whatever its means of and motive for coming to us may be, information about the possibility of global or massive disaster is useful. On a very deep level, humankind desires this knowledge. Humankind does not want to be kept in the dark. Humans therefore instinctively keep their sensors out, maintaining a protective awareness regarding past and potential cataclysms. The problem is that with this healthy instinct comes a deeply buried blindness. Even if various people do not feel themselves to be fearful, they cannot help but be affected by imagery buried deep within the collective mind. These traditionally and genetically preserved visions bring on the great fear of death.

This discussion is important in that it traces the source of our individual awareness of possible disaster back through human history and Earth history to pictures of actual disasters that have taken place and can indeed happen again. Every living thing has deeply ingrained survival mechanisms that should promote an ongoing protective awareness in each of us. But we somehow translate this high and pure awareness down into a lower emotional state that clouds the intelligently protective consciousness.

Many people bring awareness and acceptance of the reality of global, solar, galactic and even cosmic cataclysm down to the personal level. As a result of this instinctive translation, they start seeing potential apocalypse everywhere around them. Protective awareness and blinding fear are then mingled. Perceptions are clouded and very subjective. This is how personal apocalypses, real or imagined, are tailor-made for us by our subjective perceptions of our experiences and of the information we have regarding possible upcoming experiences. These personalized apocalypses include and confuse real and imagined, global and local, population and personal, as well as major and minor traumatic life experiences.

And to further cloud the issue, as problematic as this confusion is, it contains within it some degree of honesty. A child screaming in pain on the other side of the planet is felt on some level by a sensitive person standing here. Just knowing this suffering is taking place somewhere—no matter how we come to know this—allows us an awareness of suffering. Yes, on some level all of us are always in touch with the sensations being experienced by members of our own species, wherever they are, and even by other life forms everywhere. Some breastfeeding mothers have discovered this sensitivity—when their babies are screaming, even when out of earshot or way across town, it can cause them to drip milk! We are all this sensitive, whether or not we recognize it. This is a basic survival mechanism—sensitivity to the needs of the species.

Personal apocalypse consciousness is a reality, whether or not a person is conscious of having it. Population pain is personal suffering, even when this translation is entirely subconscious. Yes, we share the experience of pain, just as we share positive experiences.

Positive Apocalypse Consciousness

Apocalypse awareness is with us. It would be dishonest to say that intense experiences, challenging transitions or events that may be perceived as terrible will never take place. But it is also dishonest to say that there is no positive way of seeing these events. Positive apocalypse consciousness is essential. This constructive view and use of our instinctive apocalypse awareness will purify the application of protective awareness and reduce the odds of its mingling with blinding fear. Positive apocalypse consciousness is a state of knowing how to admit to oneself the difference between blinding fear and protective awareness, and how to resist labeling one's sensations as one or the other of these fears when others label them for you.

Positive apocalypse consciousness also involves a sense of rising to meet the challenge of any transition, of any death. Seeing a purpose, a positive outcome, as a distinct possibility—even if that positive outcome is simply that one can make it through an ordeal—is essential. *Endings Are Beginnings* therefore works with some basics of this positive consciousness.

Allow the ideas offered here to dialogue with your own heart, mind and soul. Try the ideas on; test them in daily life. Question as much of this as you feel driven to. Honest questioning and ongoing dialogue are means of discovering truth for yourself and for all of us. And this is the surest route to knowledge: your knowledge, our knowledge, species knowledge, living knowledge. Fear, if read with understanding, is a signal. We must learn to read our own and others' fears for their meaning. We must learn to prevent fear from blocking us, disturbing us and withholding from us our abilities to navigate change and transition—even physical death—to a new place, a higher state.

Chapter 3

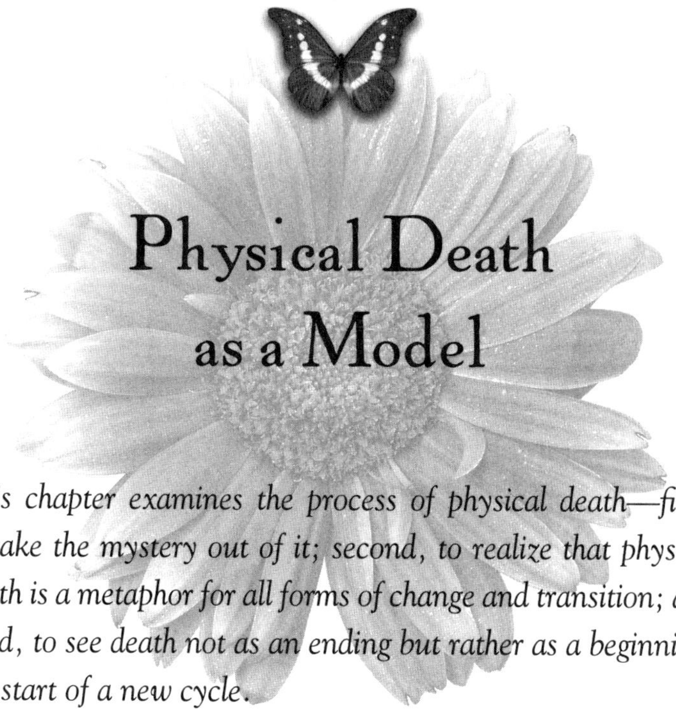

Physical Death as a Model

This chapter examines the process of physical death—first, to take the mystery out of it; second, to realize that physical death is a metaphor for all forms of change and transition; and third, to see death not as an ending but rather as a beginning, the start of a new cycle.

The possibility—and reality—of physical death is for many the greatest subject of fear. Of all shifts and changes we may tend to resist, the perceived permanency of physical death makes it all the harder for some people to digest. Yet it is the fearful perception of death rather than death itself that is feared. Death is so very misunderstood. How can we live when we do not understand death, which is such a major part of life?

So let's get right to it. Let's talk about what many consider to be the "real thing": physical death. No use waiting until we are dying to prepare—let's start now. Given that we accept physical death as one more transition in the ongoing cycle of life, perhaps one of the most (if not *the* most) profound transitions, why not prepare for it all our lives? Why reach a physical death without having prepared for it all along? This is not morbid thinking, nor is it a troubling fascination with death. Rather, this is a healthy, realistic and elevated approach to an event that we all face and for which all of life's other transitions can prepare us. In fact, the way we live, the way we master the transitions we undergo in our lives, will maximize the roles we play in our transitions out of our own physical bodies.

Death Is a Metaphor

No discussion of endings and transitions as being small and large deaths can go on without some review of the phases of actual physical death as experienced by human life forms. This is not only because physical death is what is most commonly thought of when the word "death" is said, and not only because physical death is the profound process we generally refer to when we say "death." It is also because physical death is a fantastic metaphor for many other endings, crises and transitions.

You will see the value of this comparison between physical and other forms of death as you read on. Try not to allow a fear of death or the sense that "this has nothing to do with my life right now" to stop you from stepping deeply into this chapter. It is safe to wander here. All your transitions, especially the more difficult ones, are quite similar to physical death. See what parallels you can find!

Conscious Dying Is Your Right

Each and every physical death is different; however, there are general similarities among them all. Some of the variations in the dying process relate to the style of death one chooses (if one takes the opportunity to choose, that is).

Now, contrary to what most of us have been taught, there are choices in death. As suggested earlier, this statement is not intended to balk at societal rules regarding suicide and euthanasia. That analysis is for another discussion. Again, readers' views regarding suicide and euthanasia are their own and are not contested here. Instead, another concept is being set forth: You have the choice to educate your consciousness about dying. In fact, conscious dying is your right. It is important to know how to stay connected to your consciousness while you die. Whether or not you are deemed medically conscious at the time, you are still deemed "medically" dead.

Getting to Know Consciousness

Let's be clear about consciousness here. Being conscious by medical definition may not be the only way of being conscious. There is some form of ongoing consciousness whether the person is medically conscious, in a coma or in another state. Consciousness is really a continuum rather than an on/off state. In fact, even in a "waking, fully conscious" state (so-called by medical terms), there are overlaps between levels of consciousness [see Figure 3.1]. And even in a waking state, we may think we are more conscious than we are—or less! Let's just assume that there are degrees of consciousness even in so-called "unconscious" states.

There can even be degrees of consciousness, not only in waking life, not only during the dying process, but also once what appears to be physical death has taken place. First, let's talk about biologically based consciousness. If some degree of biologically based consciousness lives in each and every cell of

- **Where are we in daily "waking" life?**
- **Where do we *think* we are in daily "waking" life?**
- **Where do we appear to others to be in daily "waking" life?**
- **Where do we appear to others to be when in various phases of physical death?**
- **Where do we appear to ourselves to be when in various phases of physical death?**

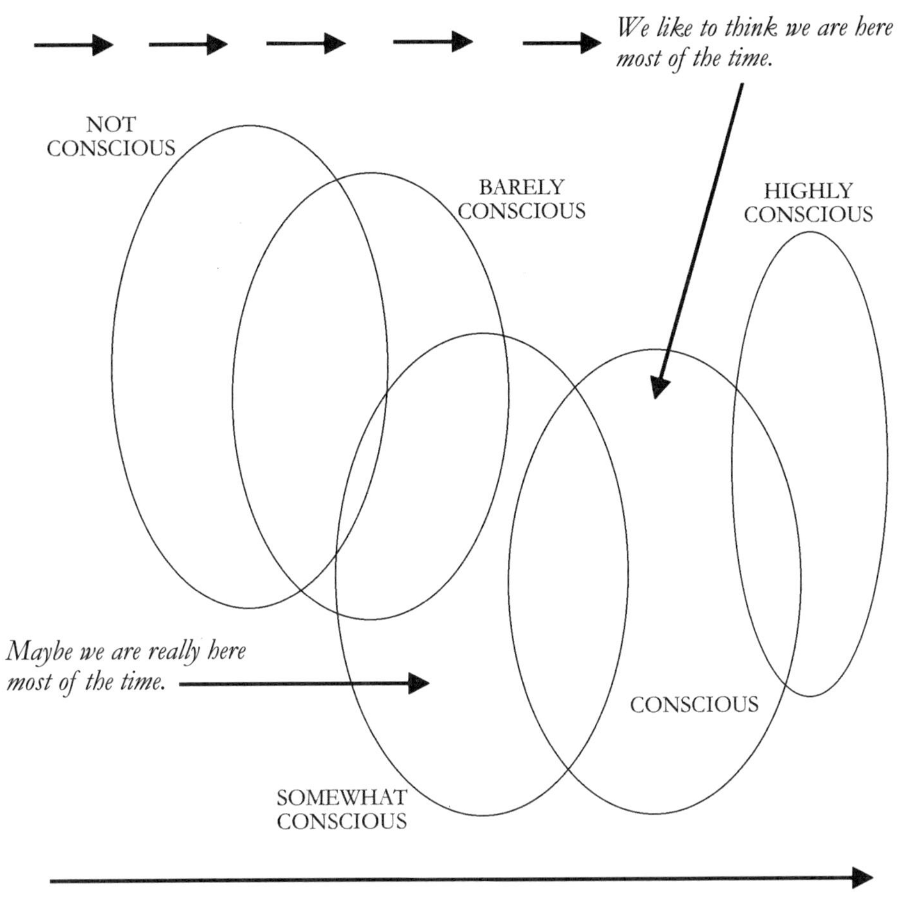

Figure 3.1. Overlapping levels of perceived consciousness.

the body, then the aspects of the consciousness that are biological may not die all at the same time. Whether or not it is agreed upon that this is the case, it is increasingly clear that the physical body does not die all at once. Modern science is discovering that many a body appears dead and is pronounced dead while what may be billions, even trillions of its cells are still alive. Some medical theories propose an immediate lowering of the nearly dead and even already pronounced dead body temperature to just above freezing, inducing a sort of hypothermia, to allow the cells to reoxygenate and to refurbish themselves.

While modern medicine continues to blur its own line between physical life and death, more theological and spiritual studies of the mind and soul have long done and continue to do the same thing in very different ways. We really have no way to prove in scientific terms that the consciousness dies. A heartbeat and a brain wave are not means of proof here. We cannot prove that there is nothing beyond the physical using physical and medical measures.

Think of the old story about the sailboat heading for the horizon. You are on the shore, watching. It appears smaller and smaller as it moves away from you. Eventually you can no longer see that sailboat; it has crossed the horizon. This does not mean that sailboat has disappeared out of all existence. All this means is that you cannot see—with your eyes—the sailboat. You cannot say the sailboat has sailed out of existence.

Now imagine that your dying friend is moving away from you, "dying" as we call it. This friend is leaving the physical body, crossing over—crossing the horizon line between the physical reality and the reality beyond. This person's once biologically based consciousness moves away from you like the sailboat. But this does not mean that the consciousness is out of existence. You cannot know this by looking at the body it was once tied to with your physical eyes, which were developed to see in this physical dimension. There is no proof that the "dying" person's consciousness is anything but past what you see (from where you stand) as being the horizon.

So the consciousness crosses over. This suggests that the consciousness can remain in existence even if you do not see it doing so. The consciousness has the option of crossing over—alive, well and conscious. This is all the more reason to instill as much consciousness as possible into one's understanding of the dying process—in fact, to prepare oneself for conscious dying—and all the more reason to understand that conscious dying can take place whether or not a person is medically defined as being in a state of consciousness, semi-consciousness or unconsciousness.

Medically defined consciousness is focused on biologically based consciousness. We are focusing on something else: the consciousness beyond this, the consciousness that crosses over. We might want to think in terms of the transfer of control—the physical body houses, or perhaps borrows, the consciousness for a while (during the physical lifetime) and then returns it to its nonphysical home. Or perhaps the consciousness always lived there, beyond the physical realm.

For Those Who Question, Call This Metaphor

About now, if not earlier in the reading of this book, there will be readers who question this thinking. This is perfectly acceptable. In fact, this is most desirable. All that is presented here comes in the form of ideas to be tried on, thought about and traveled around with. Much of what is presented in this chapter has been culled from discussions with medical, theological and indigenous specialists and doctrines, as well as from close work with persons who were near or in the process of dying physical deaths.

Questioning is good. In fact, questioning may allow an inquisitive mind to take all this in, in the form of metaphor. Metaphor is a wonderful teaching tool. In this case, we want to be able to apply the metaphor of physical death to all changes, transitions and endings we experience in life. We also want to take what we learn from living deaths to our appreciation of physical death itself, and metaphor is the vehicle for the transmission of this knowledge. Imagination is triggered when we put our minds to work on metaphors. Imagination has opened many doors. So where believing is not experienced, simply imagine. Call all this science fiction if that will allow for the consideration of the possibilities presented here.

Death Comes in Steps and Phases

Although they do not entirely correspond, several different phases of death have been described by members of both the medical and the spiritual fields. Reducing these down for simplicity's sake, we can say that there are at least three phases of physical death (although physical death has increasingly hazy boundaries) and then additional phases past what is recognized as physical death. We can think of these in terms of the death of the physical body and its biologically based consciousness by degrees (from a more medical perspective), or the death of the physical body and then the transition into a different form of the less physical components of the self and its consciousness (in more spiritual terms, although there are at times overlaps between medical and spiritual explanations of these phases). Merging the medical and the spiritual phases of death and expanding upon them, we arrive at an interesting place: We can see death both ways at the same time [see Figures 3.2 and 3.3].

Note that the dying process does not necessarily begin when an individual is given a certain amount of time to live, or when an individual contracts a "fatal" disease or injury. Medical doctors do not necessarily see their "dying" patients as "dying" the very moment they begin dying. We might say that the death process is ongoing, and in many cases, perhaps most cases, is undetected for a very long time. We do not know when most dying processes begin. From some perspectives, physical death begins when we stop growing, when we become adults. This would mean that we spend most of our adult lives dying. Every day we live, yes, but every day we also die a bit.

Generally speaking, medicine will tell us that we actually begin the dying process itself when the body begins to physically shut down, little by little quitting its physical activities. Some say that when life support is administered to save a life, it is an interruption of the dying process to save that life. Of course, life-support systems are not only utilized to save the lives of dying people. Sometimes life support extends a life, sometimes it eases suffering, sometimes it helps family members who wish to do everything they can for a dying loved one to feel that they have. And sometimes doctors put patients, even dying patients, on life support to protect themselves from lawsuits that might argue that the doctor failed to do everything possible to save the life and therefore did not save the life. Motivations for the use of life support come in many forms. It is a good idea for each of us to give serious thought to what we want done for and to us

* We are so much more than meets the eye.
* Who we are and where we are is something the physical eye may not tell us.
* What dies when the physical body dies?
* What does not have to die?

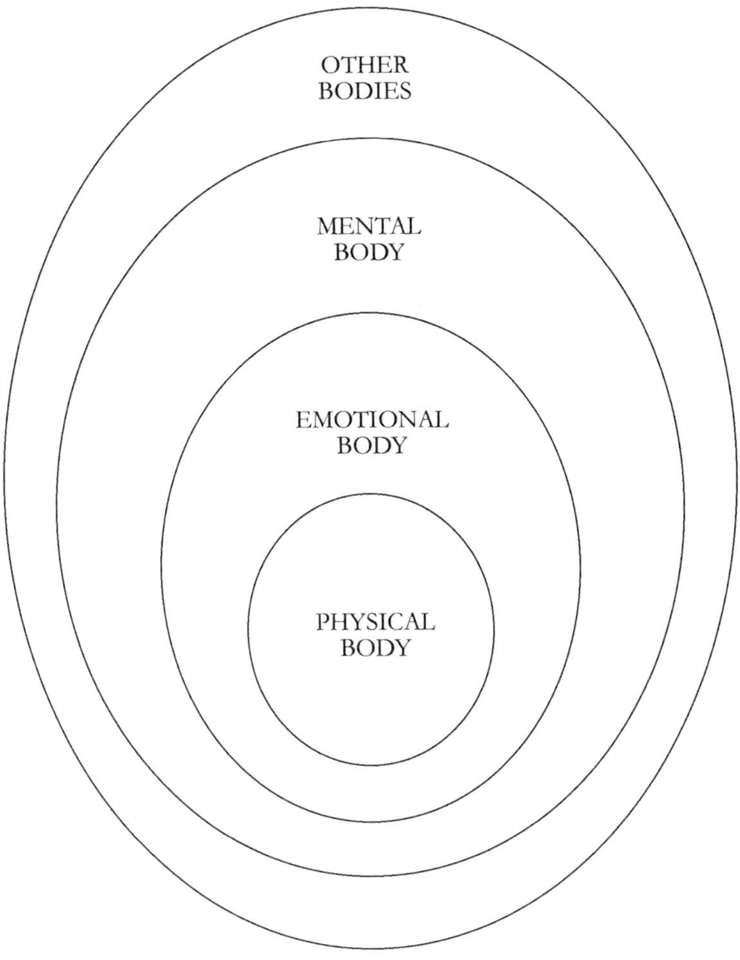

Figure 3.2. Our many bodies.

Physical, biological death involves the stages of the separation of the life of the being from the physical body, with a common pattern of physical death proceeding as in the three phases of biological death listed below. Non-biologically defined death or transition typically involves departing the physical body and the emotional body, and moving into the bodies that are not biologically based. These non-biologically based bodies may be retained or shed.

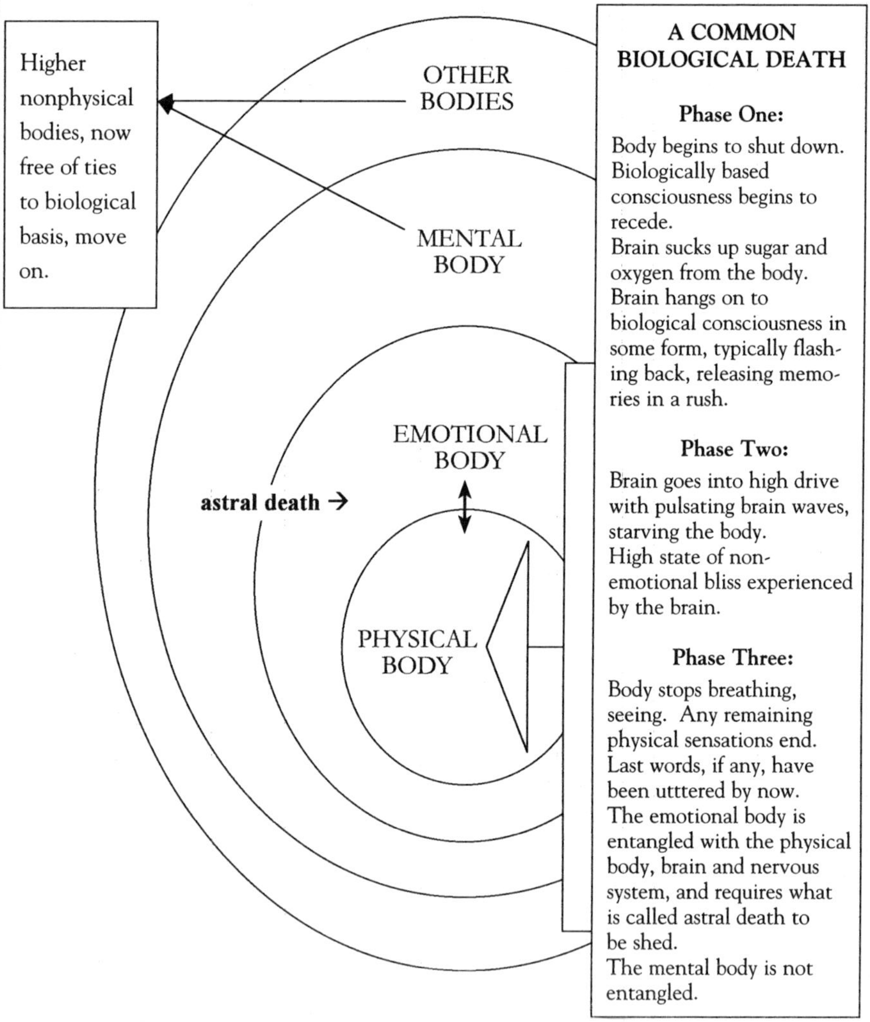

Figure 3.3. Coordinating phases of death.

while we are undergoing phases of death, and make this clear to our doctors and loved ones well in advance.

For example, quite often (but not always), the first phase of actual physical dying is said to be experienced semiconsciously. Whether or not it is, the dying person can nevertheless be more conscious than he or she may appear to be to medical personnel or other onlookers. Some piece of the mind, the self and/or the soul is present. Moreover, quite often, early in the dying process, blood pressure substantially reduces. The brain therefore finds itself running short of its normal supply of oxygen and sugar. So the brain turns on a compensatory mechanism that dilates its blood vessels and draws extra blood from wherever it might be stored in the body. This gives the sugar-hungry brain a brief increase in its blood sugar. The brain hangs on to its biologically fueled inner consciousness in this way.

At this point, the brain is, for a brief time, receiving an enriched supply of food. With this increase in brain food, the dying person is able to flashback or even to rapidly review his or her entire life. Some form of consciousness is actually intensified here, although little emotion is felt in these flashback moments. This is because this intense review is a higher cognitive activity, with little (if any) involvement of lower emotional processes. It is distinctly possible that the metacognition can be trained to navigate this process whether or not the physical body is medically conscious. The extension of this notion is that the metacognition may be active and may be trained to be yet more active after the physical body has been left.

At this time, the brain, mainly the cortex, is working at a feverous pitch. Now it is consuming sugar faster than it can get it. This results in the brain's sensing that it cannot continue to fuel the intense flashback process. When this awareness is registered, the brain begins moving into the second phase of physical dying. The brain can be operating at a very high frequency now, maintaining rapid rhythmical beta brain waves with some spurts of alpha. This can generate what some human meditators can bring about for themselves without dying—a sense of bliss, a transcendent sense.

Whether or not appearing to be conscious in medical terms, the brain is in its way conscious of this state of euphoria or intense happiness. Yet this is not really an emotional experience in the way we experience joy in daily life. This is a very special, very high state of emotional bliss.

This phase of physical dying draws to a close. Up to this time, medical or other efforts to revive the dying person, to return the dying person to the mortal body, can still be successful. Many a dying individual, persuaded by this profound euphoria, is committed to dying by now. Most physically dying persons at this point want to die this physical death.

You Have a Right to Move On

Remember that when you find yourself in this state, you do have a right to move on. You can choose the timing and nature of this step for yourself if you have taught yourself to know this. And in reality, we all know this already. We just need to remember.

Given that there has been a long social training to prevent our knowing this (how to die consciously and at will without committing suicide), we may need assistance remembering. It is therefore best to begin remembering before encountering physical death, to give ourselves little trainings about and notes for the future, and to do this in the now. Every transition offers practice in moving from one phase to the next. We can allow our consciousnesses to see the parallels, and practice—even master—these living transitions and eventually physical death.

At this point in your dying, it is going to be important to remember that you can still easily make a conscious decision to either go ahead and die or to come back into your body. You can actually make this decision without medical intervention pushing you in either direction. You are quite powerful at this juncture. You just need to know this at the time. You are rarely told this, even though this knowledge is your birthright.

Crossover Sensation

If the dying person moves on into what is called in medical speak "death," the third phase of physical dying begins. Now the body will stop breathing and the physical eyes will stop seeing, although the eyes have most likely stopped looking before this time. The brain will stop running, as it is out of sugar, and will choke on its waste matter. The dying individual is quite aware of these sensations in a detached and neutral way.

The last words, if any, will have been uttered—usually mumbled or whispered—by now. One of the last physical sensations is the feeling, again not unpleasant, that the mouth is filled with cement. This is actually a physical sensation and is likely far more than only a physical sensation. Here is where the crossover sensation is experienced just about as tangibly as anything this ethereal can be. The cement filling the mouth is actually the cement of the ether, the nonphysical reality, flowing in.

This is a complex sensation in that the feeling of cement suggests something thick and heavy, something very physical.

But what is heavy is the physicality that is being left behind. The sensation of cement filling the mouth is three things:

- One, it is the awareness of something we have been feeling all along throughout our physical lives: an awareness of being physical and therefore being weighed down with physicality. Separating from physicality gives us, perhaps more clearly than ever, awareness of the tremendous thickness and weight that physicality—even the slightest bit of skeletal physicality—gives us to carry.
- Two, the cement is also the coming of a numbness to the tactile and sensory functions as these have been known in the physical body. One of the last sensations felt is the sensation of no feeling, numbness, a bit like the anesthetic felt at the dentist's office. And the mouth, being close to the brain, may still have enough fuel to feel the physical numbing.
- Three—and what makes all of this yet more complex and wondrous—the contact with the nonphysical dimension (the ether, as it is often called) is being made. Although this other dimension is always present and available to us, we are not necessarily alert to its presence. Even when we are alert to its presence, the billions of micro-mini sensations coming to us at all times when we are in a physical body tend to drown out the ongoing flood of pure etheric essences that we are always in touch with and swimming in without realizing that we are doing it. Now physical sensations retreat, diminish and then fade away, and in flows the reality.

Crossing over into nonphysical reality has many characteristics, but for now let's simply say that this crossing is a splendid experience. Learning about it in advance is a wonderful way to train the consciousness to watch for these steps and to take them adeptly and consciously.

"Oh Look, I'm Still Here!"

The ether is not material in the sense of the three-dimensional reality the dying person is leaving. The ether is more airy, if air can be something nonmaterial for the purposes of this discussion. The ether is the realm into which the dying person is now moving. Once this transit is completed and even during this transit (without medical intervention calling the individual partway back), there will be no further physical sensations unless the dying individual chooses and believes, or imagines, there to be.

Imagines? Well, yes, imagining here is tricky, because the imagination cannot arise from the shut-down physical brain at this point. Most persons who are able to be somewhat conscious during this time will sense, feel and imagine that they are not in their bodies. Some will feel that they are concurrently in their bodies and out of their bodies. The sensations of the body may linger, in a somewhat parallel way to a person who has lost an arm or a leg but who still feels sensation in that lost limb, as if it is still physically attached. Remember that this is a good time to observe how much of your sensation of reality you can conduct with your mind, whether or not you have a functioning body or working sensory organs.

Now there is a continued awareness of self and the chance to look at the body that is being shed. Some people see someone kissing their soon-to-be physical corpses and experience a detached longing for a physical body again. Others, most, are rather relieved, even profoundly relieved, to let go. Remember to stay conscious here.

You can stay conscious here. Practice in daily life and notice when your mind is seeing, feeling, thinking. Observe yourself being conscious. Get to know your consciousness; dance with it. Hone your metacognition. Learn to stop regularly and take the time to notice your location in what you have been calling space and time. You are mapping your reality, your higher reality. And you are training your consciousness, your metacognition, to map its reality.

Freeing the Soul

Letting go is critical here. You should remember that you can stay conscious as you do so. It is important to understand the letting go or severance process. Physical death is the withdrawal of the soul from its primary anchors: the heart and the pineal gland in the brain. This withdrawal from the heart and from the head cuts off the two streams of energy that unite the ethereal soul with the physical body—with the bloodstream and the endocrine stream or system. This cutting-off severs the connection between physical body and nonphysical soul.

Sometimes a body resists the departure of the soul that has inhabited it, and then this severance process may be slow and messy. It might be better said that some souls, not understanding this process, do not fully cut these cords, these energetic strings that can to some extent be pulled across the dimensions. If you stay quite conscious here, you can choose to cut these cords—these umbilical cords—for yourself and deliver yourself into a new dimension of reality. You can give birth to your new self here.

Now you are virtually finished with physical or medical death. But there is more. Once you pass out of the body or physical vehicle, you have passed from the first episode of death or the first death, which is physical, to the second death, which is not physical. In this next death comes what some call the astral death—the death of the emotional vehicle. You have grown quite a large and complex emotional body during this lifetime!

Meanwhile, once the physical house of the body is truly empty, it begins to decompose. It may even begin to decompose before physical death takes place, which is a situation the dying person may not want to be tied to. There is a distinct irony here. On the one hand, cells may live on beyond the moment the body is declared physically dead, and on the other, the body may be decomposing before the body is pronounced physically dead. The dying of cells and the living on of the body has taken place throughout the life of the body, but as physical death comes, these processes are out of sync from a physical standpoint. Every day we are living and dying; this is all part of an ongoing process.

You may want to think that death is complete at the physical end, after the phases of physical death described above. Yet the next dying, the astral death, is just as much of a great passage, if not more so. The individual who has just lost her or his body may still retain many of the ties or cords to feelings and awarenesses of others' feelings that were acquired while in that body.

A highly trained being can leave the physical and the emotional vehicle quite consciously and, in full waking awareness, preserve the continuity of consciousness while moving from the physical plane to the after-death state. You can do this whether or not you have received intensive training, so long as you stay conscious (remember, we are not talking about staying biologically conscious here) and remember that all your feelings are part of an emotional body that you are shedding. If you stay stuck, trapped in your emotional body, your consciousness, energy and power weaken.

Those who do not understand this second stage of death—emotional death—may enter it hysterical, fearful, angry and/or bewildered, and may needlessly waste their spiritual energy. Try to take this information in by studying it from time to time. You will remember bits of this description many times during your living and dying. You may want to read a more intricate review of the physical dying process than we have space for here.

Letting Go

Eventually, whatever her or his awareness, the physically dead individual must leave behind all emotional connection to the physical plane and move on. This letting go is a critical and somewhat difficult process for many a consciousness or soul. At this point, the consciousness—or perhaps even the soul—senses that what can come after emotional-body death is the dissipation of any remaining biologically attached or corded mental energy. The mental body can linger after the emotional energy has been shed, or it can die the death of the mental body, the third death.

It is said that very few spirits are "evolved enough" to succeed in fully completing this third death and, by doing so, crossing the threshold beyond the death cycle. It is also said that most fail at this death and therefore must recycle again and again until some day when they will finally succeed. We ask you to be alert here and question this particular message. It is not wrong; however, the surrendering of one's mental energy must be studied closely. When you die this third and final phase, where does your mental energy go? Where do you go? Do you want to go there? Are you willing to stay conscious right on through the very challenging death process in order to look closely at where you are sending your precious human energy at this juncture? Do you know you can choose what you do with your mental body and with your consciousness? Can you imagine a reason you might not have been told this?

Navigating Death

You must navigate your death consciously in order to avoid surrendering your mental energy—energy you cultivated during your physical lifetime—to a force that may use it in a way other than the way you would freely choose to have it used. Each of us must assume responsibility for remembering this. If you can accept this responsibility, you may be able to help free countless souls from being prisoners cycled through the human energy plantation and other farms and factories such as the one on Earth throughout the cosmos.

Whatever conscious focus on moving through the physical (or actual) and emotional (or astral) episodes of death is achieved by the dying individual will serve as great training for the soul. The intelligent, survival-oriented road map from physical to astral to mental death is one drawn by repeated exploration of the process. Navigating the three deaths well is the greatest challenge for a being. Recognizing the major choice you have regarding your mental body is essential. Being aware of choices helps you to access them. Reminding or guiding others who are undergoing physical death, whether or not they are medically conscious, can help these others access choices at death. On a broad population level, we have been denied much of this awareness, and now is the time to take this awareness back. You can choose to be part of this expansion in awareness. You see this option, then someone else sees this option, and then more of us see this option.

A Question of Rights

Here is the metaphor: Navigating one's death is a process. There is an art and a science and a politic of dying that we can learn and that we can apply to all types of transition.

Your right to die consciously and in the manner you choose for yourself must be exercised while you are on Earth and in your physical body as well as in the period after you leave your body. Human rights extend far beyond the physical plane, including post-physical consciousness. You, as a consciousness, can exercise your rights there—if you so choose.

Chapter 4

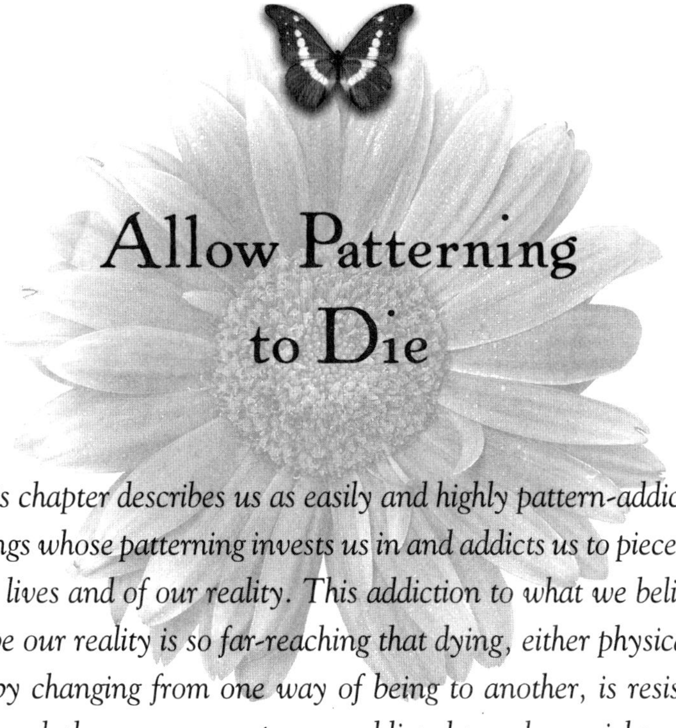

Allow Patterning to Die

This chapter describes us as easily and highly pattern-addicted beings whose patterning invests us in and addicts us to pieces of our lives and of our reality. This addiction to what we believe to be our reality is so far-reaching that dying, either physically or by changing from one way of being to another, is resisted in much the same way a person addicted to a drug might resist breaking this addiction. Addiction to a reality is a form of resistance to both conscious death and positive transformation.

We frequently describe ourselves and each other as "creatures of habit." We can indeed see ourselves as fleshy robots—nice, soft, cuddly ones maybe, but nevertheless programmable biological machines. In fact, the genetic programming we are born into and the programming we absorb (burned into our brains and nervous systems as we live in our environment) determine a great deal of who we are. The neural programming we accumulate during our physical lifetimes has such a heavy influence upon us that it can be immensely difficult to erase. In fact, the most certain erasure of the neural programming may be the death of the physical body and its physical nervous system. This is why the concept of death is so central an issue in terms of personal change, behavioral change and life change. Some things have to die out in order for new things to begin.

This explanation is included at this point in the book in order to explain that a healthy "death"—even a death within a life, such as the death of a behavior—can eliminate undesirable programming. Falling far short of actual suicide, we can continue to live while allowing parts of our lives to fade away, die off and be replaced. Why do we not just understand this and change more readily and enthusiastically? Because we are the creatures of habit we act like.

Our perceptions of our realities, our ways of being and all our behaviors carry elements of the habitual. So why don't we understand that change is not easy because we tend to be addicted to the way things are? We (both as individuals and as a population) tend to try to preserve the status quo. Living, even surviving in physical bodies in this physical plane relies on our tendency toward pattern addiction. So the very characteristic that helps us survive kills us. The following discussion of pattern addiction—a sort of self-induced or self-allowed brainwashing—is essential to our understanding of the difficult time we have with many changes and deaths. We are addicted to what we think is our reality. We feel that dying is losing a reality to which we are hugely attached.

Our Rigid Addictions to Life as We Know It

There is more to our resistance to death than the blinding fear of the known or unknown and, alternatively, the protective awareness. There is also a deep, genetically ordained drive within every genetically coded living organism to become addicted to patterns. This is, for the most part, a survival-oriented tendency. After all, it is essential that we respond automatically and rapidly, without taking the time to think, to life-threatening situations. It is also convenient that certain necessary behaviors become habitual. How many people would stop their cars at red lights on time if they had to take the time to figure out from scratch each time what the red light signifies? It is very good that we program ourselves to do some things automatically. However, there is a downside to this automatic programming capability of ours.

Seeing how rampant some very obvious problematic addictions have become, we recognize the downside of patterning. In recent times, humans have become increasingly conscious of the problem of addiction to destructive and dangerous patterns, such as compulsive overeating and compulsive sex, as well as compulsive drug and alcohol use. These are what we can call *explicit additions*—obvious, visible addictions. These behaviors tend to be more easily recognized than other more hidden, more *implicit addictions*, such as the very obscure but very powerful addictions we have to our ways of life and realities. Yet explicit addictions are basically only symptoms of implicit addictions to deeper behavioral, emotional and energetic patterns.

Implicit pattern addiction, even when life-threatening, does not always signal its presence through explicit addictions. It can be very difficult to detect. Implicit patterning can make its presence known in a variety of ways that we do not always connect back to the patterning, such as chronic pain and disease. Even deeper than that is the source pattern addiction that drives all other addiction [see Figure 4.1].

Explicit (Surface) Pattern Addiction

↑

Implicit (Hidden) Pattern Addiction

↑

Underlying Source Pattern Addiction

Figure 4.1. Layers of pattern addiction.

Clearly, pattern addiction is both a positive and a negative part of the human condition. Pattern addiction comes with the genetic package, which is supposedly survival-oriented. So can we concern ourselves with our hidden pattern addictions? Yes! This is the message here: The more prepared we are to detect and transcend detrimental behavior patterns—even, and especially, the hidden ones—and to let them die out, the more active a role we can play in our emotional, physical and spiritual health, and therefore, the more free will we will have.

Unseen Implicit and Source Pattern Addiction

Most implicit pattern addictions are built over a long period of time, constructed on the deep foundation of the source addiction. While we may literally inherit some of this addiction—receive it through time from deep within our genes—much of this addiction behavior is taken on once we interact with our environment. In fact, most everything we carry in our physical genes must be activated by the environment. Even being conceived and then born involves interacting with the physical environment, or physical plane as we may also call it. Geneticists call this interaction the genetic-environment interaction (GE) and have indeed touched on at least some of what this is about. I say "some" because there is much more to the directions life forms receive than what is measured in laboratory analyses.

Our bodies run themselves via their own internal electric companies—their own nervous systems. Most of our neurological programming involves the establishment of electrical and energetic patterns throughout the body. This programming takes place over time. Such patterning becomes detrimental when harmful to the emotional, physical and/or spiritual well-being of the individual (or family or community or society or globe). Pattern addiction frequently manifests itself in explicit symptoms, such as the destructive addictions to drugs and alcohol named above, and also in physical pain, chronic ailments (including ulcers) and sometimes even serious physical diseases.

Some pattern addiction is so subtle, so very implicit, that it involves hidden rigid holding patterns restricting, directing or entirely blocking the transmission of necessary electrical charges as well as full blood flow and ample oxygen to remote parts of the body. "Remote" here refers to nerve endings, organs, brain cells and other tissues of which we are often unaware. "Remote," then, does not signify physical distance here; it signifies distance from consciousness. Therefore, the more aware one is of something, the closer one is to it. For example, tight musculature or tissue surrounding digestive organs can interfere with the transmission of oxygen and neurological impulses involved in building or using digestive enzymes. Tight musculature in the head and neck can lead to jaw grinding. Damaging energy patterns can make a body sick.

Rebalancing Is Not Always Enough

Most afflictions are the product of problematic or troubled energy flow patterns. A rebalancing or correction in the transmission of patterns of neurological energy throughout the body can reduce and even alleviate many health problems. When this rebalancing is brought about, a harmful energetic pattern—the implicit pattern of the affliction, physical pain or illness—is broken. This pattern, or at least its surface program, has died.

However, to effectively eliminate the negative impact of the deeper aspects of this pattern, it must be taken through a complete death and extinguished. Without correcting the underlying and more implicit pattern addictions—without overriding, overcoming and then erasing the power of the programming behind the troubled physical and psychological symptoms—the same or similar symptoms can continue, recur and expand. The deeper problematic pattern behind the surface problem pattern must go.

However, surgery will not erase this, nor will pills or general medical interventions. Basically, interventions of and from the physical dimension of the problem will not address the nonphysical dimension of the problem and the nonphysical elements of the deeper underlying source pattern. This inability to permanently eliminate deep patterns is of course largely due to the inability of current medical and psychological technology to see the layers of patterning driving a large part of all behavior and dis-ease. Yet each of us carries internally the gift of ending patterns from the inside: a kind of internal shedding that must take place.

The knowledge allowing us to do this is already within us. We must travel through the surface patterns down to the implicit patterns and down to the source patterns driving them.

We know how to will ourselves to undergo a thorough transformation—even a complete overhaul. We just need to be reminded how. All we need to be able to do is travel deep enough to the place where we can let underlying patterning die. In this manner, we can die and heal, and die and survive!

Substance Addiction as an Example

Let's travel back up from source patterning through implicit patterning all the way to the surface: the explicit patterning and addiction we can see. Drug and alcohol or substance addiction offers one of the most tangible examples of explicit patterning. Persons addicted to substances move from "triggers" that bring out in them reflexes, urges and even cravings to repeat again and again the behavior of the addiction patterning, which brings out in them the use yet again of the drug to which they are addicted. Until the pattern of this addiction is broken, the person trapped in it remains just that: trapped. A new response will interfere with the patterning, providing at least an insight into an alternative to this pattern; however, it will take substantial work to hold that insight and break this deeply burned-in pattern. Breaking this pattern would allow the new response to be the new way of life, as diagrammed in Figure 4.2.

Substance addiction also offers some of the most tangible evidence that addiction to a pattern can indeed be transcended. Substance addiction is therefore the primary, but not only, example provided in this book. You can see the parallels between substance addiction and all our pattern addictions.

Substance addiction is everywhere. Let's examine the societal implications of this threatening explicit addiction so common in modern times. Many illusions surround substance addiction. One

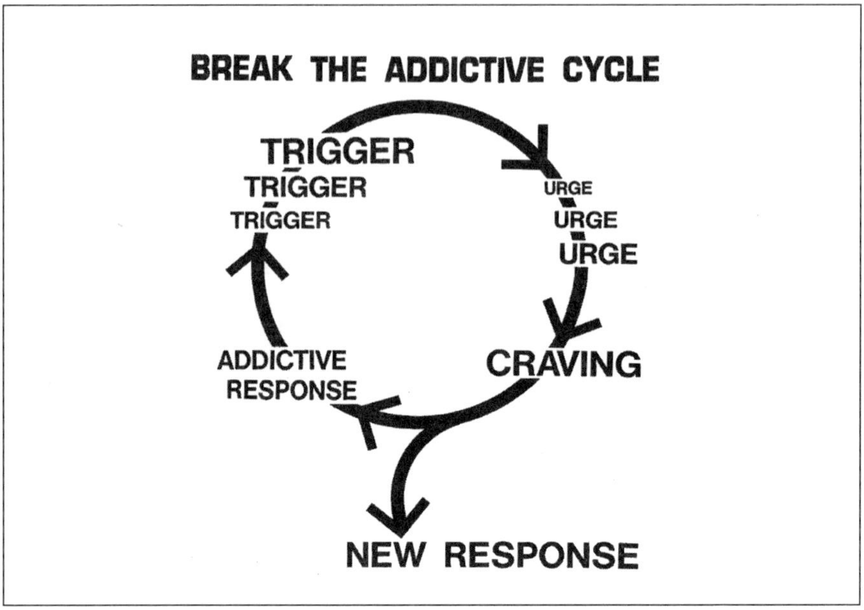

Figure 4.2. Breaking the pattern of addiction.

is the illusion of health. Far too many addicted individuals are in a state of denial about their health problems. Too many claim that they are not addicted and use their seemingly good health as proof that they are not addicted. But their lives are wounded, caught, tangled in the damaging machinery of detrimental patterns. These people are operating under the illusion of health, as well as under the illusion of not being addicted. Most people who suffer from any sort of detrimental pattern addiction are in a state of denial about its danger and severity, if they admit to its existence at all. This denial is often part of the programming.

It is not only the addicted individual who generates illusions; the surrounding social machinery does so as well. Look at the medical model and its communities—they operate under the illusion that addiction requires "treatment" and that the forms of truly medical treatment provided are appropriate for fully treating the addiction. However, pattern addiction is not a symptom that can be medicated, it is not a tumor that can be cut out and it is not a sickness that can be fully treated by traditional medical practices. Succumbing to detrimental patterns such as addiction is an immensely complex matter—one presenting a serious crisis of the will, the heart and the soul. It is evidence of the very real possibility of the diminishing of free will, even the death of free will, as individuals succumb to or lose themselves to submission to deep root-level source programming.

The Death of a Pattern Is an Opportunity for Transformation

In this crisis of the will, the heart and the soul, is the possibility for transformation and for the transcendence of detrimental patterns through the death process. (Note that "transformation" and "transcendence" are not typically listed as courses in medical school syllabi. This is largely because many do not understand their profound relevance in healing.) Crisis is opportunity—opportunity for attention, learning, transformation and transcendence! Most people wait for a major psychological or physical crisis to begin to even vaguely address their pattern addictions.

In the drug addiction treatment world, this crisis is sometimes called "hitting bottom." Hitting bottom can compel addicted or otherwise afflicted individuals to seize the opportunity to learn and to care about their mental, physical and spiritual health. Hitting bottom is a call to action. It is also a call to either let old behaviors die or just physically die. Many people who think that they have never been detrimentally pattern addicted to a substance or to a behavior or to a relationship or to something else have not experienced this opportunity.

The drug- and alcohol-addiction treatment communities do reflect some understanding that the crisis of addiction provides the opportunity for transformation. A great deal of work with addicted persons involves spiritual work. It is important for other arenas of the health care community (of which the addiction treatment community is but one part) to recognize addiction and all forms of afflictions as opportunities for transformation, and to seek to bring about that transformation.

Overhaul Is Key

Part of this recognition is the embracing of the reality that addiction to detrimental patterns affects health. Breaking pattern addictions can heal a variety of maladies, even diseases. Hitting bottom, crashing into a sort of death, can be utilized in healing afflictions. When addicted or ill individuals arrive at any treatment or medical service, program or facility, they should find themselves at the door to mental, physical and spiritual overhaul. To walk themselves through such a doorway—one into true overhaul, to really do it—is to die a death into greater free will and freedom, free of patterns that made them sick, past the death of these patterns. Here is the threshold of transcendence. Here is the opportunity to harvest the death of the negative patterning for the very energy needed to be free from it!

All too often, addicted and otherwise afflicted individuals find themselves standing at the door to anything but health. Most mental and physical health care services manifest a range of attitudes toward affliction, but they rarely say, "Welcome. We are fortunate to have you among us, because you are about to lead us in an exploration of the deepest level of self—mind, body and spirit. You are about to meet the challenge of addiction to hidden patterning, to understand the death of one's patterning, and in that understanding, to help explore the frontiers of healing, of freedom, of human potential, of healing potential and of the human soul. We are truly fortunate to have you among us."

Instead, addicted and even physically ill people are subtly labeled, implicitly stigmatized and treated like "sick people." It is not so much a lack of expertise that is the problem with most mental and physical health care; it is a lack of understanding what so-called "sick" individuals are all about and a lack of respect for the critical role that they play in the evolution of human consciousness. Like canaries going ahead of miners in a cave, testing the air for breathability, reading the signs of danger, people who feel ill give us signs. And people who heal their illnesses indicate that there is a way to survive the cave, or to find a new path out of the cave to a new place.

The Tension in Our Addiction to Reality

Working toward a closer look at our addictions to our realities, let's continue using drugs and alcohol—substance addiction—as the path to understanding. Our species both creates and experiences two primary addiction conditions, conditions applying to each and every one of us. We have heard so much about the "drug and alcohol problem" in modern times. However, we tend to overlook the fact that all of us are potential, even actual, substance addicts.

Indeed, substance addiction is a crisis, not only for the addicted individual, but for everyone in our society. We need to better understand this crisis, as it teaches us about what is happening to all of us. It signals the tensions emerging in two major areas of modern existence. These tensions are in fact real areas of addiction affecting all of us living on this planet today. For where any one of us may view herself or himself as being entirely free of the two key conditions discussed below, none of us truly can be because the human race is not.

Overarching Addiction Condition One: Chemicalization

Reaching beyond the boundaries of individual bodies and psyches is our broad and inescapable modern-day species-wide dependence on chemicals. Let's call this overarching addiction condition *chemicalization*. Slowly, man-made chemicals are filling our air, our water, our food, our bodies and our minds. Our homes are cleaned with detergents. Plastics are everywhere—we wear them, we play with them, we drive them, we may ingest them even when we try not to. Medicine says it offers chemical solutions to many of our health problems. A reliance on manufactured chemicals has become a way of life in our modern world.

As a result, we are all to a great degree chemically dependent. We are all pattern-addicted to the chemical world. What a trap! What a paradox! Substance-addicted people, singled out as the only chemically dependent ones, are making the reality of everyone's increasing dependence on chemicals more apparent. Yet they represent the tip of the iceberg.

Overarching Addiction Condition Two: Mechanization

Also reaching beyond the boundaries of individual bodies and minds is the overarching addiction condition we can call *mechanization.* Not only does the increasing mechanization of everything we do affect our lives, but it also affects our definitions of ourselves. Every day we feel either indirectly or directly the increasing mechanization of our realities.

Slowly, almost invisibly, we are surrendering our individual freedom. We are acquiescing to the reality of what we can call numbership—a reality in which we identify ourselves as a series of numbers (telephone, social security, driver's license, tax identification) and mechanical processes (checking in and checking out, registering, paying, driving). Without even seeing it happen, we are beginning to treat ourselves as numbers, machines, items, things. The effect of mechanization on our perceptions of ourselves reaches into the deepest recesses of our psyches, unbeknownst to our consciousnesses. It is ironic that contained in the word "numbership" is the word "numb." As we become more like machines, we actually become numb to our humanity.

And here is the alarm going off: Many addicted individuals claim they want to "numb the pain" of their existences by using drugs or other substances to "turn off." We are learning more about our behavioral switches and our use of these. We know that some of us are addicted to the chemical switches we call drugs. Yet this is more than just some of us. We all treat ourselves like machines with on/off buttons.

Just about everyone has turned to painkillers to dim or switch off headaches, body aches and injuries. Check the inside of your medicine chest. Can you toss out its contents without hesitation? We mechanize ourselves without even realizing it. What switches do you use? How frequently do you treat yourself like a machine?

Chemical switches are part of our modern (and even our

ancient) lives. So are electrical switches (such as television) and emotional switches (events we rely upon to change our feelings). These emotional switches include parties for energy or happiness, music for sexual arousal or relaxation, holidays for loneliness or comfort, disagreements for neurologically registered anger or righteousness, and full-blown arguments for adrenaline-driven violence or other tension release. As you can see from this partial list, turning to switches is not, in itself, bad for us. What is problematic is the way we use switches on ourselves, plus the tendency we have to rely on them, to run on automatic like machines rather than pay attention to how we are turning events, emotions, objects and chemicals into switches and ourselves into things that can be switched on and off.

How Pattern Addictions Control Us

When a globe full of societies grows alarmed about things like drug trafficking, smuggling across borders, narcoterrorism and drug addiction, it is responding to surface, explicit problems. And yet there is an unspoken, intuitive understanding of the implicit spiritual ramifications of such explicit problems. Something about the deepest level of the human condition is being expressed.

Chemical dependence is only one expression of a far more common and more harmful behavior that afflicts much of our society—destructive dependence. The reality of human existence is that a "little addict person" lurks within all of us. To better understand this little addict person we all share, we can frame this issue into two key concepts: addictive materialism and addictive inadequacy.

Destructive Dependence Number One: Addictive Materialism

One way to look at explicit addiction is to see drug- and/or object-addicted people as materialistic, material reality-addicted people—which is virtually all of us. We will reach outside ourselves for a material thing—a sort of mechanism, a car, a house, a television, a computer, someone's body, food, or in the case of our primary example, a substance or drug—as a way of working with our own internal psyches. For example, if we feel depressed, we may take a drink, a hit, a pill, a shot or a line. We depend upon an external material item or experience to rescue us from an undesired internal state of our mind. Of course, our state of mind may reflect external predicaments—things going on in the world around us—but our ability to cope with those predicaments is not really based on any continual process of interacting with those predicaments. Instead, it is naively based on a concrete external item or object, usually to be taken or experienced physically.

The substance- or object-addicted individual's preoccupation with a material world item or experience serves as an escape from the more arduous task of really dealing with feelings and situations. In a materialistic society, we are conditioned to depend on a material substance or experience in order to avoid the pain of actually living through and learning from a crisis.

Destructive Dependence Number Two: Addictive Inadequacy

During the 1960s, that era's so-called drug users openly claimed that they were turning on and raising their consciousnesses through the use of mind-altering chemicals. Although some may have succeeded in their consciousness-raising efforts, others—perhaps without being aware of it—were actually trying to turn off and to diminish their consciousnesses. This kind of user has come to rely on drugs (including alcohol) to take the jagged edges off the harsh realities of life.

In this picture of substance addiction, individuals use drugs simply because they cannot cope. They feel that their own psychological coping mechanisms are inadequate, insufficient in the face of the pressures of modern life. This sense of inadequacy drives much compulsive behavior; it is in no way limited to persons who are drug- or alcohol-addicted.

These Addictions Apply to All of Us

These two explanations point to the global nature of addiction. The problems of addictive materialism (dependence on outer means for solving inner problems) and of addictive inadequacy (a habitual response driven by a sense of not being able to cope) are common to a greater portion of society than the mere population of those addicted to drugs and alcohol. How many of us go shopping and end up overspending when we are bored, depressed or faced with a crisis? How many of us have trouble dealing with the realities of life and are forced to depend on externalities?

Not all of us are addicted to dangerous chemicals, but we all exhibit signs of addictive materialism and addictive inadequacy. Each of us regularly seeks to compensate for these source-level addictive characteristics within ourselves. This means that the addicted individual is not alone and not unlike the seemingly not-addicted person. We all have a great deal in common. If we are honest with ourselves, we will admit that we have seen the pattern addict, and he or she is us.

How We Form Pattern Addictions

What we do here, in this physical dimension, has effects far beyond the physical reality we think we know. Pattern addictions, whatever their symptoms, trap energy. Repeated loops with no obvious exit wear on those who travel them. Be careful how you use your energy, whether it is physical, emotional, financial or spiritual energy.

Pattern addictions sneak up on people. Underlying source patterning is fertile ground in which to form surface addictions: As above, so below, and as below, so above. Take, for example, the development of a drug or a relationship or any other surface explicit addiction. These standard addictions do not begin explicitly. You may even be in an addiction pattern right now and not realize it because the pattern is not yet an explicit addiction.

Let's back up a moment. An addiction to a drug or a specific behavior usually begins with casual behavior. Casual behavior is light, experimental, seemingly without deep consequences. The experimenter lives in a society that appears to allow at least some degree of freedom to experiment and explore. "Try this just once, then decide if you want to try it again," or "I dare you to try this. Come on, show us what a man (or woman) you are." Experimenting is a part of growing up and self-discovery. But sadly, much casual behavior becomes regular behavior, and explicit patterns are born.

Casual Behavior → Regular Behavior

EXPLICIT (SURFACE) PATTERN

↑

IMPLICIT (HIDDEN) PATTERN

↑

UNDERLYING SOURCE PATTERN

Always as this movement from casual behavior to regular behavior is taking place, there is a deeper source pattern fueling the process. At some point, some regular behaviors become a bit too regular, too repeated. The easy ability to stop the behavior reduces. The regular behavior can thus become a troubled behavior, again always fueled by the underlying, more implicit source pattern.

Regular Behavior → Troubled Behavior

EXPLICIT (SURFACE) PATTERN

↑

IMPLICIT (HIDDEN) PATTERN

↑

UNDERLYING SOURCE PATTERN

People who are exhibiting troubled behavior continue a behavior even in the face of its adverse effects to themselves, their health, their minds, their work, their families, their businesses, their neighborhoods or their societies. It is easy to slip from regular behavior to troubled behavior, because the early signs of troubled behavior are subtle and often go undetected. Again, consider substance abuse and dependence as a blatant example. Someone who has a few drinks at a bar on the way home from work is likely already going to be driving under the influence—however slight that influence may be—of alcohol. Of course, driving home may be entirely possible. The point is that many users who are in a state of troubled behavior do not consider the risks that their use is posing to themselves or to others. They are not even aware of how easily they can slip from troubled behavior into full-blown addicted behavior.

Casual → Regular → Troubled → Addictive Behavior

EXPLICIT (SURFACE) PATTERN

↑

IMPLICIT (HIDDEN) PATTERN

↑

UNDERLYING SOURCE PATTERN

Fortunately, not everyone who uses alcohol or other drugs, overeats, gambles or engages in compulsive theft travels this tragic path. Some of these persons—these "casual users"—try a behavior once and then consider the experiment completed. But all too commonly, casual users unwittingly slip into becoming regular users. They confidently tell themselves, "It can't happen to me. I'm too much in control of my life to develop an addiction to anything. I'm just having a little fun."

In reality, we are deluding ourselves. Case history after case history demonstrates that casual problem behaviors, without training regarding how to avoid programming oneself, dramatically increase the probability of developing fully addictive behaviors. And any behavior conducted regularly increases the chances of its being programmed into you. This is an explanation of the descent into detrimental pattern addiction. Any behavior can be expressed once or twice. Yet somehow we can too often be blind to the crossing of the boundaries between casual and regular, regular and troubled, troubled and addicted. Why? Because we are genetically programmed to slip, unaware, into pattern addiction almost blindly, whether it be a negative or a positive addiction—unless we are highly watchful.

The Freeing and Right Use of Our Energy

Is this genetic tendency to acquire programming mere happenstance? Is it the misfiring of the survival-oriented function (designed to have us respond automatically to falling boulders, red lights and other safety signals)? Or are we prisoners of a source mechanism buried deep within our coding—a mechanism rendering us readily programmed creatures of habit, almost eager to succumb to automatic behavior?

Are we prisoners of coding that tells us to live pattern-addicted and then to die? Compulsive addiction to drug consumption, food consumption, sex consumption and other consumptive and repetitive behavioral patterns—while being unaware of the effects—can actually make us emotionally and even physically ill. Such pattern addiction is life-threatening. Some people physically die of detrimental addictions without first breaking these addictions. We must be conscious in order to be able to catch ourselves slipping blindly into negative patterns.

Chapter 5

Move Death into Pattern Transcendence

This chapter recasts death as an opportunity for pattern transcendence. Understanding the phases of transcendence and being able to detect, identify and navigate them allows us to harvest our minor and major deaths for higher states. In life, we become addicted to the very programming we shed in death. Thus we tend to fear and even resist this shedding. When this shedding—this death of our patterns—finally takes place, it is a healing event.

Breaking a pattern is a form of dying. In fact, all dying is a breaking of patterns, and all breaking of patterns is a form of dying. Are you prepared to die, to transform old patterns into something new? Are you ready to transcend any detrimental automatic, habitual behaviors and perceptions? Will you succeed? Can you let these behaviors and perceptions die off?

Transcending One's Programming

To die well, to bring about a worthwhile living death, you must break your addiction to the programming that controls the pattern you are talking about changing, even if the pattern is your life. Those concerned about chemical dependence, painful relationship patterns, chronic pain, physical diseases and other crises of one's programming are working with the same questions: How can one break out of an addiction to one's programming? How can one break away from the underlying source coding directing the creation of pattern addiction, even of pattern addictions that are not good for us, are dangerous for us, or are sometimes even lethal? What type of death will you require to release, to free yourself?

The only difference between the obvious and the more hidden pattern addictions is that some addictions to programming are more subtle than others. The drug-addicted individual sees a physical thing, a drug, to which he or she is addicted. Individuals dealing with repeated emotional or physical health patterns often have no physical objects (with the exception of their own bodies, in the case of dis-ease, and the body of a relationship partner, in the case of a habitually troubled relationship) onto which they can project or externalize their patterns, which makes the problem-process of addiction to one's underlying source programming much more difficult to recognize.

The first step is to again and again face the reality that addiction to patterns takes place in all of us. Explicit addictions serve as great learning vehicles. Like the tip of an iceberg, they make the hidden components of pattern addiction more apparent to us. Implicit and even source addictions are sometimes discovered and unearthed by people who are in recovery from explicit addictions or who are fighting serious physical illnesses. These individuals become examples for all of us. They lead the way through the matrix of death into the realm of transcendence.

Conditions for Transcendence

Many of our problems are actually encountered or created to provide us with the opportunity to transcend them, to heal our lives. As human beings we have a choice: we can either become so overwhelmed by our problems that we miss out on this amazing opportunity, or we can realize that even the deepest pattern addiction is a potential-laden situation.

Those who are addicted to a pattern (of drug use or eating or something more subtle, such as an emotional or energetic pattern) have a wonderful opportunity to experience transcendence—specifically to transcend pattern addiction. Transcendence requires a new outlook on a situation. No matter how bleak and painful a situation might appear, it can be changed by perceiving it differently. This means that before any changes can occur, you must be convinced of the fact that you can turn things around. You must believe in the possibility of transcendence. You must also understand the phases and process of transcendence, which must be studied continually. No matter what level of understanding you reach, there is always more to be learned.

Remember, there is no such thing as a free lunch. Transcendence can be hard work until you get the hang of it and until you see the larger picture—the map of the process. The transcendence process requires your commitment, your attention, your fortitude and your faith in the process. These are interactive states of mind.

Phases of Transcendence

Transcendence is a continuous process through which an individual can achieve elevation to higher and higher levels of awareness—what we can also call spiritual planes. There you will experience greater awareness and a higher degree of freedom. Transcendence is composed of four profound phases, each of which is necessary for the process. These phases of transcendence are:

Phase 1: Struggle
Phase 2: Paradox
Phase 3: Insight
Phase 4: Spiritual Elevation

Each phase has its own special characteristics. You will find diagrams of these phases within this chapter. As you examine each diagram, try to think of your life in terms of it. Make these diagrams part of your own mental imagery. Thinking about complex ideas in simple pictures often helps to learn about them on a deeper level.

Phase One: Struggle

Minor and even major struggle is so common that we frequently do not see its full presence or actual nature. We may struggle with other people, with family relationships, with work relationships, with ourselves, with morality, and maybe also with our cravings for drugs, with balancing our checkbooks, with heavy traffic, with our health, with our tempers, with our moods or with living up to what we think we should or what others would like to see us live up to.

We often struggle without recognizing the struggle, or we recognize the struggle but cannot see beyond it. We can become so deeply caught up in struggle that it becomes impossible to step back and say, "Oh, I am struggling. This must be the first phase of transcendence." But it is just this observation that will set us on the path to transcendence. When we are struggling, we must take the time to tell ourselves that we are struggling and recognize that this is good, because it is the first phase of transcendence.

Study Figure 5.1. This pattern illustrates the ups and downs, pushes and pulls, highs and lows so typical of the struggling phase. During a true struggle, there must be low points in order for there to be high points—both extremes are integral to struggle.

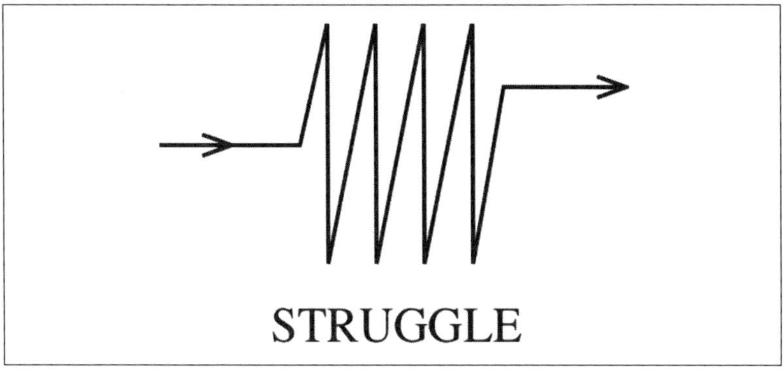

Figure 5.1. Phase one: struggle.

Phase Two: Paradox

The trap we call paradox can be a fantastic experience. It can be painful. It can be frightening. It can be deadly. It can produce a numb, zombie-like effect in those who experience it. Paradox is the experience of being in a situation from which there appears to be no exit, no escape and no resolution. The more powerful the paradox, the more a trap it will appear to be.

Recognizing the presence of paradox can be highly useful, in that every paradox presents the opportunity for release from paradox. The more intense the paradox, the greater the release from it will be. Energy trapped in paradox builds a valuable tension, unless it is not understood, not recognized and trapped for too long, in which case it stagnates and weakens. What a waste!

We all know paradox. Sometimes parents submit children to paradoxes in the form of double binds. "Which coat do you like?" a parent may ask a child. "Do you like the red coat or the blue one?" When the child says, "The red coat," the parent says, "That's not a good choice; you should like the blue one." And when the child says, "The blue one," the parent says, "Well, the red one is much better."

When this happens, the child is experiencing what is called a double bind or a lose-lose scenario. In this case, there is nothing the child can do that would be the "right thing" in order to elicit a positive response from the parent. The child is bound by unpleasant consequences no matter which choice he or she makes. There appears to the child to be no escape. Indeed, the situation holds, or so it seems, no real choices.

Some double binds come from outside us, but most come from within, because we allow ourselves to see situations as double binds. In living life, both children and adults create double-bind situations for themselves with or without the help of other people. For this child, release from the bind is seeing the folly of the parent's reasoning and not taking it personally. This is a large job for a child.

One double bind that many people find themselves in is chemical dependence. The individual takes a drug to escape a painful, stressful or boring situation. But the situation from which the person is trying to escape becomes even more painful, stressful or boring when the person returns to it, as is inevitable upon coming down from the chemical trip. While no escape is no escape, the drug escape is also no escape.

Paradoxes like this are extremely stressful and often painful. But faith in the transcendence process shows us that paradox serves a purpose. Without the tension of paradox, without the feeling of being trapped in an unwinnable situation, there is no impetus for release, for moving on, for growing. The energy of the tension created by your paradoxes, when used well, can generate enough energy for you to not only break out of them, but to rise above them. You must learn to spot your paradoxes before they stagnate in order to harvest the valuable energy from them. Without the painful tension of paradox, you cannot experience the power of release—the jump or shift in perception—that is produced by breaking out of the double bind.

Paradox is illustrated in Figure 5.2. Study it for a few minutes. It shows the "standoff" or "holding pattern" in which people get caught or trap themselves when they need to let some piece of themselves die in order to experience transcendence. The only way out of this holding pattern is to break out of it and move on, to increase your perception so that you can see beyond the limits of the double bind that holds you in place. The two arrows in Figure 5.2 that end up pointing against each other and going nowhere represent the opposing forces that hold a pattern-addicted person in his or her trap. This deadlock can hold you in its grip indefinitely. Or if you choose to escape it, to transcend it, it can provide a take-off point into another level of awareness and healing, an insight, as diagrammed in Figure 5.3.

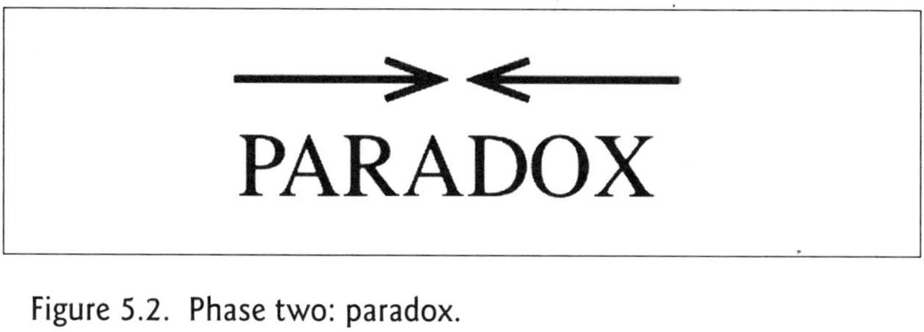

Figure 5.2. Phase two: paradox.

As has been explained above, when the paradox of pattern addiction explodes, energy is released. That fantastic energy can bring profound insight when harvested. Whatever your pattern addictions may be, you can harness the energy found in paradox and then move—fast-forward—into transcendence of that paradox. To do so, you must become highly alert to any tensions you feel, any traps you find yourself in and which of your implicit pattern addictions have generated these tensions or traps.

Phase Three: Insight

The energy released when paradox is escaped can produce great insight. Insight is a profound experience, but it often comes in small packages. Sometimes we experience insight without realizing it. For example, you may be driving along and suddenly grasp something about a problem that has been bothering you. Or you may be working—perhaps on a scientific or construction project—and suddenly figure out an unexpected solution. All at once, a new idea comes into your mind. You suddenly discover a new way of looking at a problem. This is an insight.

Insight is illustrated graphically in Figure 5.3. Look at the figure for a while. It suggests the glimpse or perception of another way of seeing the world and of being in the world. The highest point in the diagram is this flash of realization. It represents a peek (and a peak) into a higher level of experience—but only a peek. Notice that the line falls back, or almost back, to its original level. This is because insight is a temporary jump in perception. This enhanced perception is not automatically sustained. Insight does not automatically bring growth. In order to grow, insight must be recognized and sustained. When it is, spiritual elevation becomes reality.

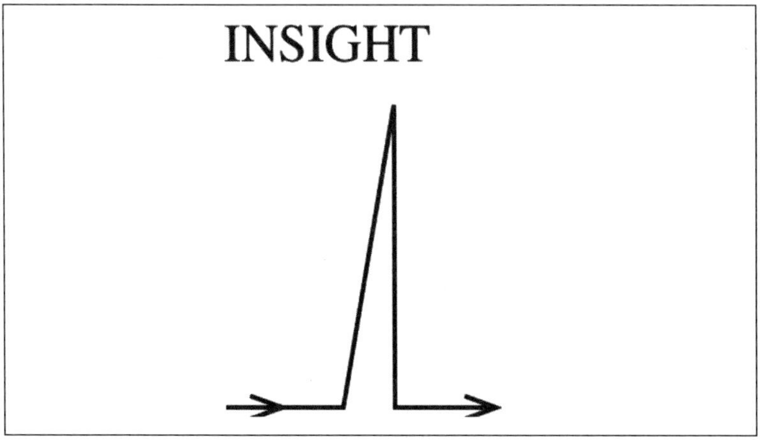

Figure 5.3. Phase three: insight.

Phase Four: Spiritual Elevation

Spiritual elevation is illustrated in Figure 5.4. Gaze at this diagram. This pattern signifies a jump in perception. This jump is actually an insight that is sustained. The self, the soul, the spirit and the consciousness itself rise to a new level of being and maintain that level. This "holding on" is best described as the experience of sustained insight. Without being sustained, the insight is usually bright and brief, and drops back to or close to the original, pre-insight way of seeing and being in the world, as is seen in Figure 5.3. Spiritual elevation differs from insight in that there is no going back to one's previous perceptions, traps and limitations.

From each new level of being achieved by each shift into a new spiritual elevation, there can be further discoveries and elevations. Each of the phases of transcendence may have to be repeated in order to reach the next level of spiritual elevation. One can always discover new struggles, paradoxes and insights to generate further spiritual growth.

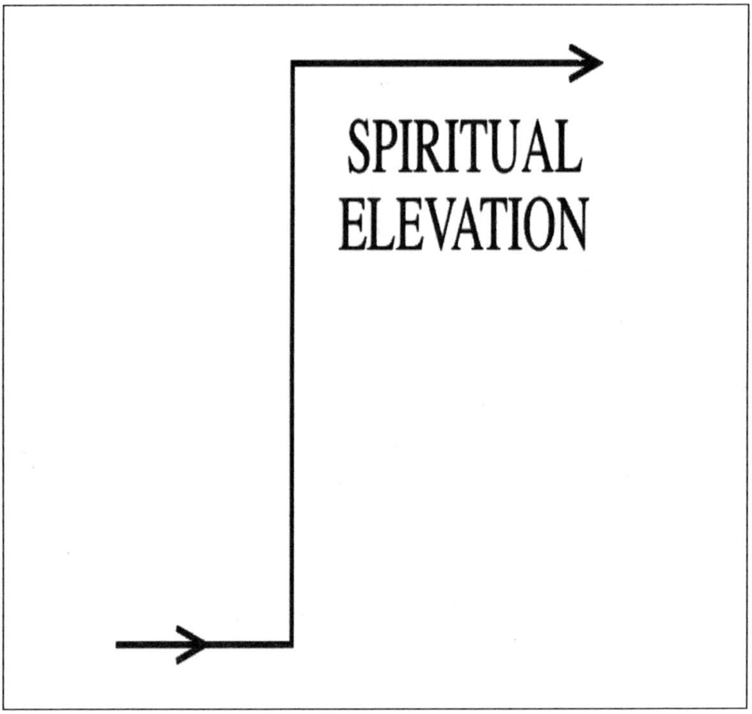

Figure 5.4. Phase four: spiritual elevation.

This exciting and adventurous process of transcendence is suggested in Figure 5.5. This figure shows the four phases of transcendence linked together, and maps a process many can live out in life. The cycle of these phases is repeatable, as in Figure 5.6. Contemplate these diagrams for a while.

Be certain that you understand that each phase may take barely a few seconds or may last for years. Some people struggle all their lives. Others live in a perpetual state of paradox. Some people have insights but do not recognize or sustain them, and thus continuously return to the same old paradox that produced these insights. Some rotate between struggle and full-on paradox with no escape throughout their lives (as in much of Figure 5.7), while others achieve at least one if not many spiritual elevations

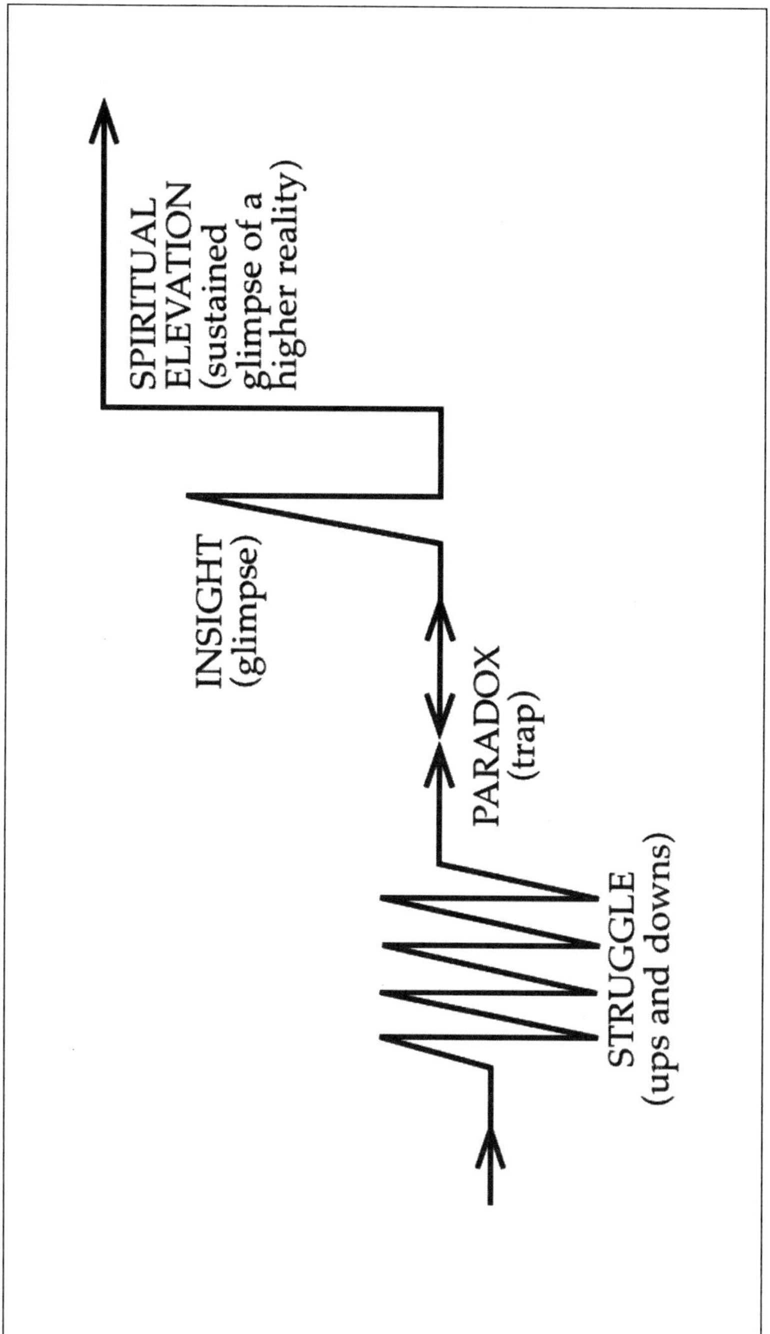

Figure 5.5. Four phases of transcendence, which can be repeated and intermixed.

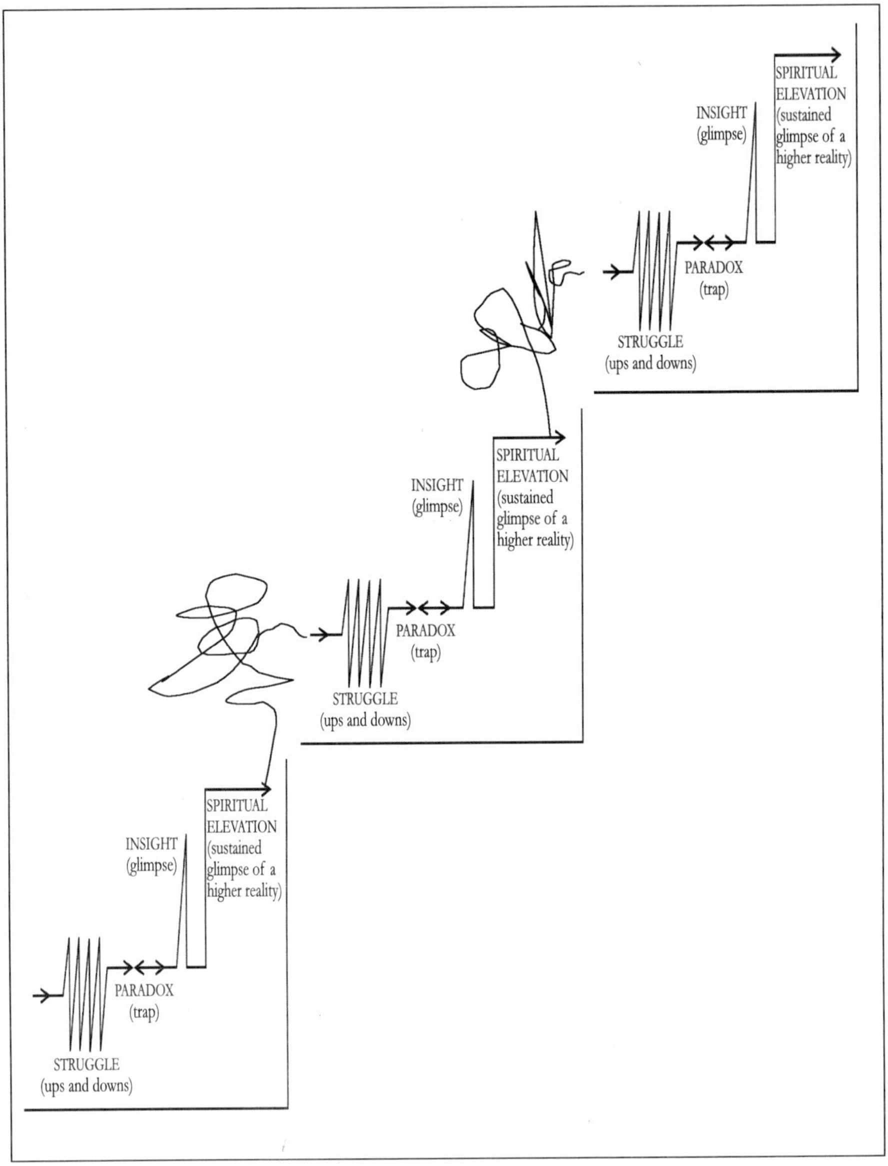

Figure 5.6. The ongoing process of transcendence.

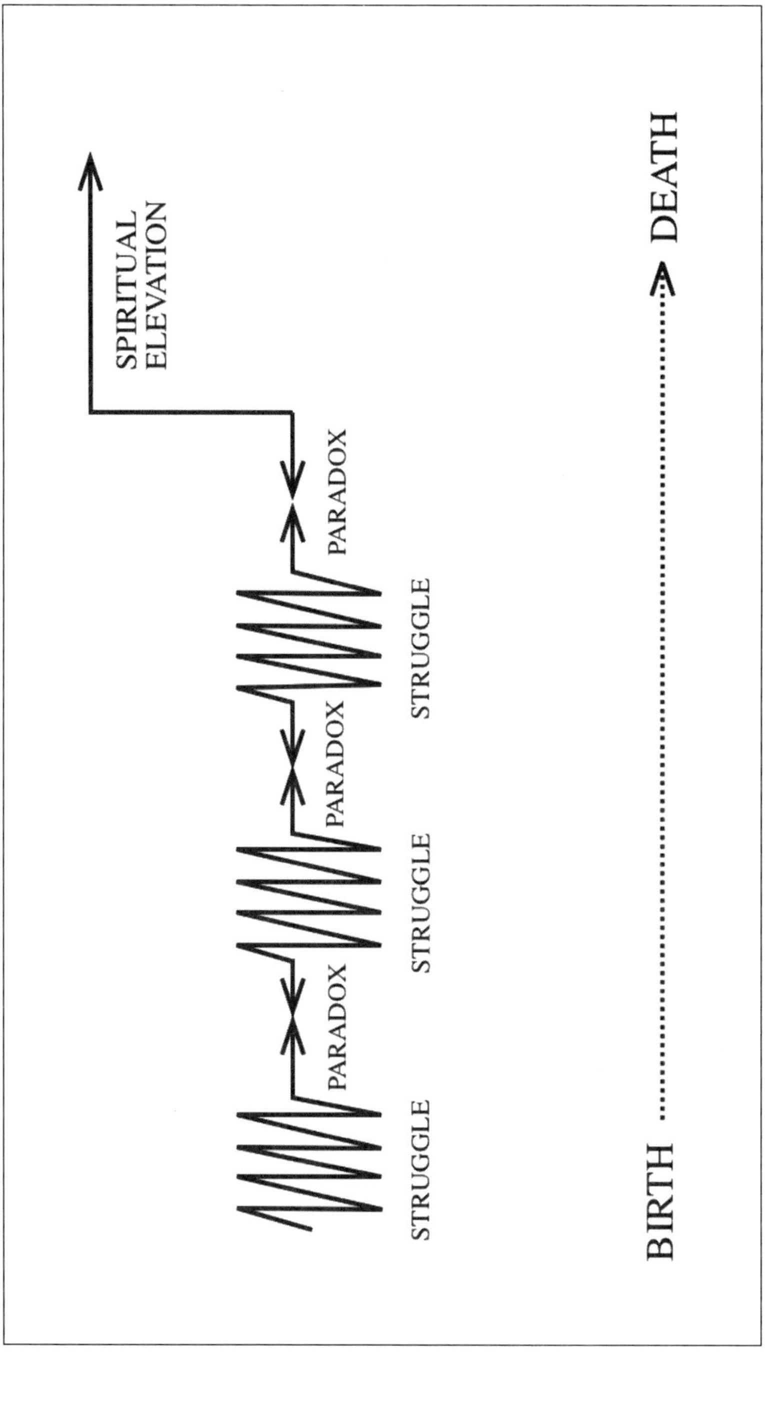

Figure 5.7. The rotation between struggle and paradox, with eventual spiritual elevation.

while still physically alive, as Figure 5.6 suggests. Perhaps these people reach spiritual elevation at physical death.

Each of us follows his or her own life pattern. Few life patterns look exactly like those seen in Figure 5.6. However, no one's pattern is written in stone. If we were taught as children to recognize the four basic phases of transcendence, then as adults it would be much easier for us to see where we are in the process and to take conscious control of it. But no matter how old we are, we can always learn to harness the precious energy produced in each phase in order to move on to the next phase. We can learn to see our struggles as fertile ground for astounding growth. We can learn to appreciate paradox, recognize insight and strive for spiritual elevation. If you continue to look for this pattern in your life, you will eventually understand that you are already on the path of transcendence. The gifts of life and death will then be clear to you. Your struggles are important stepping-stones. Respect your struggles.

Basic Ideas for Transcending One's Patterning

We have been examining the concept of transcendence—what it is and what it takes to achieve it. The concept can be applied to any obstacle or difficulty we encounter, whether it be emotional, financial, physical or any other type of challenge. Remember, even chronic and serious illnesses have a habitual pattern component, even if invisible and existing on an energy level, and even these can be transcended when transcendence is fully understood. Mastering transcendence involves the following seven basic understandings:

1. Addiction to a pattern is a powerful bondage that can only be broken by something more powerful. One must

accept this as a fact and appreciate the seriousness of the task of breaking pattern addiction.

2. Pattern addiction can be very surface—obvious and explicit—or very subtle and difficult to recognize. Therefore, some individuals either present themselves or are presented with the challenge of an explicit addiction so that they may recognize how addicted to deeper, implicit patterning—and to the still-deeper underlying source patterning—we all are. They then undergo the struggle to break out of their most explicit addictive patterns and, in the process of that struggle, experience growth. Some people have found the recognition of their addictions to be profound opportunities for growth. Drug, alcohol, food, gambling and other surface addictions are some of the easiest patterns to spot and thus offer some of the most accessible opportunities to practice transcendence and growth. Whether or not we exhibit any explicit addictions, we all are pattern addicts.
3. Transcendence of patterning is a key form of learning. Transcendence is a process composed of four phases: struggle, paradox, insight and spiritual elevation. This pattern is a repetitive, never-ending process. Your entire experience of living and dying large and small deaths is transformed the moment you identify the phase of the process you are currently experiencing.
4. Life's challenges generate the struggle and paradox that promote insight, spiritual elevation and thus transcendence. The pain, struggle and paradox of pattern addiction is therefore immensely valuable.
5. Remember that the transcendence we are describing is

a process that gains power as it progresses. Progressive transcendence can overcome pattern addiction and then move beyond it. There is no end point to this process.

6. Maintenance of progress along the road to transcendence is essential. One must work to maintain the insights and spiritual elevations gained in the process of transcendence. Knowing where we are in the process and what to seek to preserve is valuable.
7. Transcendence is never-ending. With every full cycle of transcendence comes an entirely new way of seeing the self and the world. Be ready and open to total change and new life.

Only total change and an ongoing commitment to transcendence will heal the wounds to the soul that are caused by our deep, deep addictions to our source patterns and realities. And only massive transcendence will heal us as individuals and as a species caught in too many self-destructive, freedom-stifling patterns. As the human species becomes more aware of its ability to consciously choose to transcend the trap of patterning in the physical world, it will acquire the ability to ascend to the realm of the fully conscious spirit. Biological death is not the only means of such ascendance. Many paths are available to us.

Chapter 6

Map Death

This chapter frames the notion of mapping transition and death processes while traveling them. Mapping creates an awareness of the larger picture and helps us to see events along the way, even challenging events, as steps to a new place.

When sensitivity to the phases of transcendence is refined, the very texture of life changes. Even subtle shifts in energy—the slightest oscillations in mood, minor modulations in the perceived tempo of time—are read like passages, like street signs. The feel of internal and external space is perceived in great detail where it might have otherwise been unnoticed. We become sensitized to our locations in space and time, and to our locations within our lives. We grow quite conscious of our course of travel through our lives and of our large and small deaths. We notice windows of opportunity, possible ways to escape our paradoxes, reading our realities as if we were reading changes in the weather. The nature of the paths we walk as we traverse our life journeys grows more clear.

Notice where you are and how you feel. Can you map your life? Can you map your living deaths? How about the roads leading up to those deaths? Mapping your transitions helps you see that endings are beginnings. Mapping also helps you navigate even the hardest of times.

Recognize the Fork in the Road

There are times when life brings you to a fork in the road. Sometimes you don't see the fork coming; it just appears. Sometimes you don't realize that the fork has appeared, or that you are straddling the forked roads and feeling the imbalance and tug of conflicting choices (caught in the situation of paradox, as in Figure 5.2). Sometimes it becomes clear that the fork branches in two directions, one being the road of addiction to an old life or way of life, and the other a road where that addiction can be shed and allowed to die. Sometimes you are actually dying physically, straddling the road between physical life and physical death. You come to feel that you really cannot walk both roads.

The next time you feel substantially unsettled for a significant chunk of time (whatever that may be to you), take a look under your feet. Try to see where you are in your life. Usually a choice to go one way or another is revealing itself. Will you take one course of action or another? In order for you to move, a choice must be made. Something must be shed or left behind, no matter how discomforting, troubling, sad, painful or confusing this realization may be.

Be sensitive to these experiences as you live your life. Despite the discomfort or anguish you may feel at having to make a choice to change or leave something behind, you can rejoice because you are actually at the junction of opportunity, the chance to escape from paradox. Figure 6.1 shows how the energy trapped in a paradox, in a double bind, is moving toward

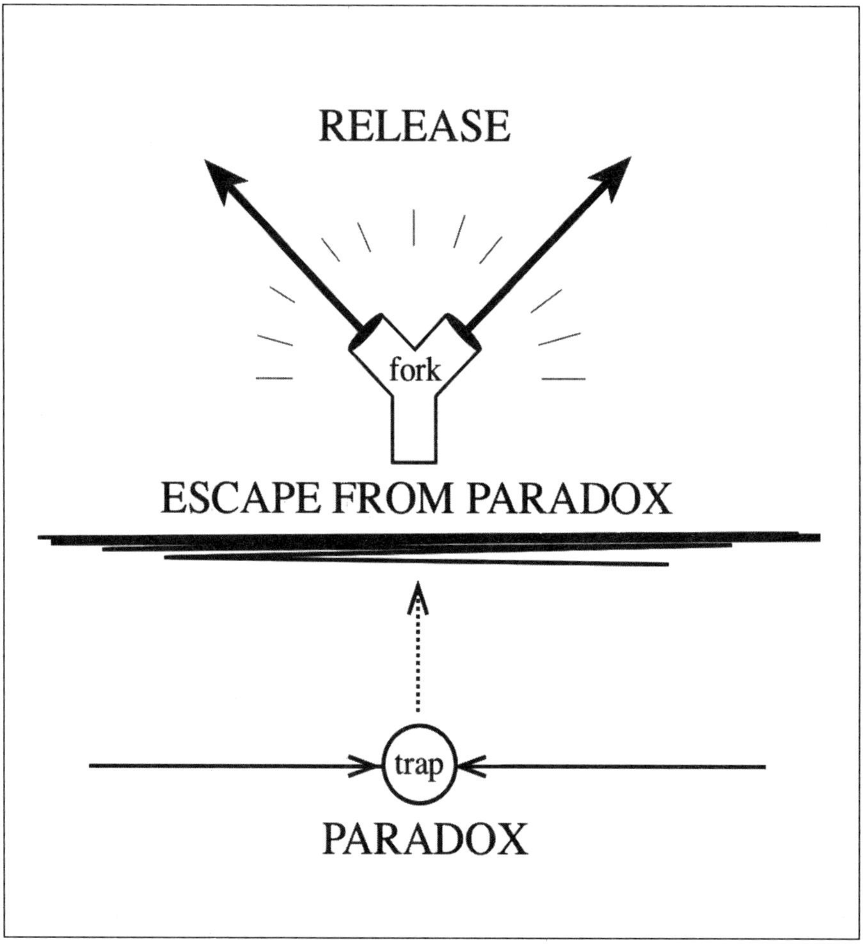

Figure 6.1. Escape from paradox.

release at the fork and how it can be released as an escape. The energy released when the fork in the road is transcended can be directed to elevate your awareness, your being.

So at the fork in the road, amidst the paradox, ask yourself: "How do I move ahead now? How do I use this situation to grow?" Choose a branch of the road. Make a commitment to go one way or the other. It is time to consciously and clearly choose to either go further with the developments already forming at the fork, or to stay the same, stuck, trapped in the inability to change. Indeed, you can choose to go back to what may be the illusion of the safer, "saner" life within the paradox. It actually can be less work to stay trapped than to break out. However, if you stay trapped, your will, your power and your energy may diminish there. Once out, you are much stronger and much freer.

Understand the Feeling of Instability

As you move toward escape from paradox, you may feel intensely unsettled. Either you or the world around you may appear to be chaotic, out of order. You may have no sense that things will ever look quite the same again. And you know that if you commit to escape, to the death of old ways and patterns, things will indeed never look the same again. And so as you commit to and then move forward toward this change, toward your growth and survival, you destabilize your trap and beat at the doors of your paradox. Now you want out, and things feel highly unstable. This is exactly the state of instability that any system, including that of a living organism (such as you), has to reach in order to evolve beyond its present level of development.

But what finally opens, loosens or releases an extremely tight and rigid trap? The more rigid it is, the more energy is required to hold it in place. Some kind of profound shift is usually required to loosen up a rigid system. This shift could be an intense realization or experience, a spiritual conversion, a traumatic or psychophysical shock, or a catastrophe or calamity. Another means of loosening up a rigid system is to clearly know what is taking place and, based on this clear knowledge, consciously navigate through it to a higher state of existence.

Hear Your Voice

Pressure to stay stuck or break free builds. About the time the pressure crescendos, you may, if you listen, hear a voice in your head. Do not be alarmed. It will not harm you. This is your higher-level consciousness, your metacognition, your higher self speaking to you. You are calling you.

Become more sensitive to the subtle input you send yourself as you grow increasingly ready to let a part of your life die. Pay attention to very quiet hints, murmurs in your mind that you would normally have missed or totally ignored. This input may contribute to feelings of imbalance, in that you might feel rather disturbed or somewhat crazy. But fear not—you are right where you should be. The holding pattern, the stability of the trap you are in, must be destabilized. Yes, sometimes it helps to rock the boat.

When you hear a voice guiding you, know that this is not craziness, not psychosis. You are transducing, reducing the frequency of the transmissions from your higher, wiser self to a frequency that your conscious mind can receive. As you gain control over your own receiving mechanisms and take conscious control of your metacognition, this process will feel increasingly natural. You will consciously be reading a wider band of information from yourself and from the world around you.

This widening of your band of perception is a marvelous advancement in the knowledge of your self and your consciousness. Still, at first, if you are sensitive enough and willing enough to hear your own voice, you may nevertheless question or even deny the experience. This is not surprising. Such evolution, especially to those poor souls who have not been instructed in the process, can be excruciatingly disorienting. To help you with this, you are now being instructed in an introductory, subtle and gentle manner. The feelings of imbalance may fade before the disorientation. However, eventually both will recede.

Map Transition

As you undergo any transition, make yourself a map. If you feel you cannot mentally visualize well, then draw the map and keep it handy. Be ready to revise or add on to the map as you continue on the journey you have begun. Some people adjust their maps daily. The following maps [Figures 6.2–6.5] represent personal change, transition and dying processes, processes of both living deaths and physical deaths. These maps are for you to explain to yourself. This is to be a form of self-instruction. Study these maps. Attempt to describe a process of change, of transition, of dying, that fits each map. Then think back to a few major changes that have occurred in your life and map the process leading up to, moving through and leaving each of these transitions.

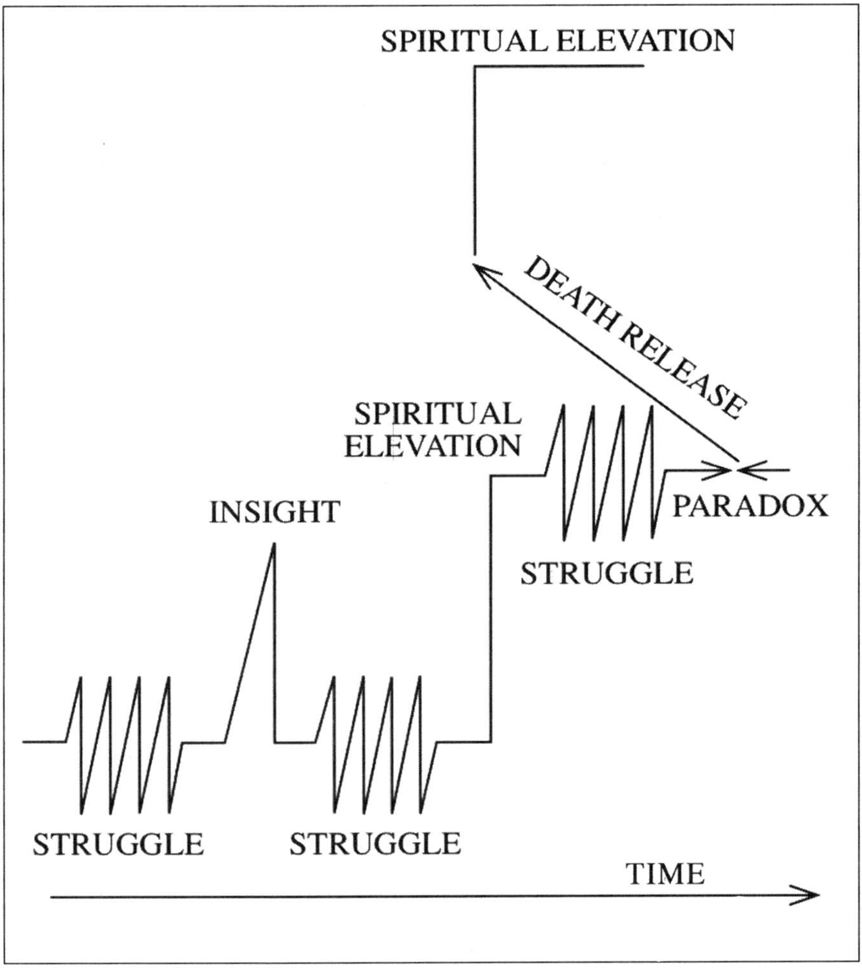

Figure 6.2. Death map one: basic death release.

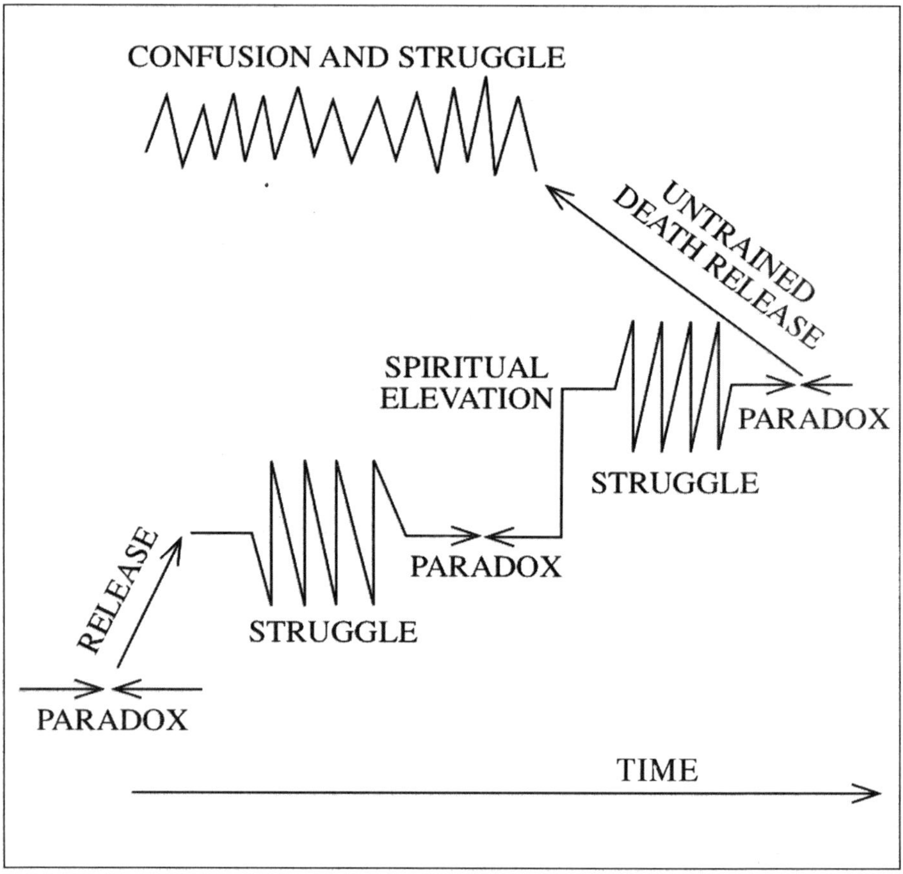

Figure 6.3. Death map two: death with untrained release.

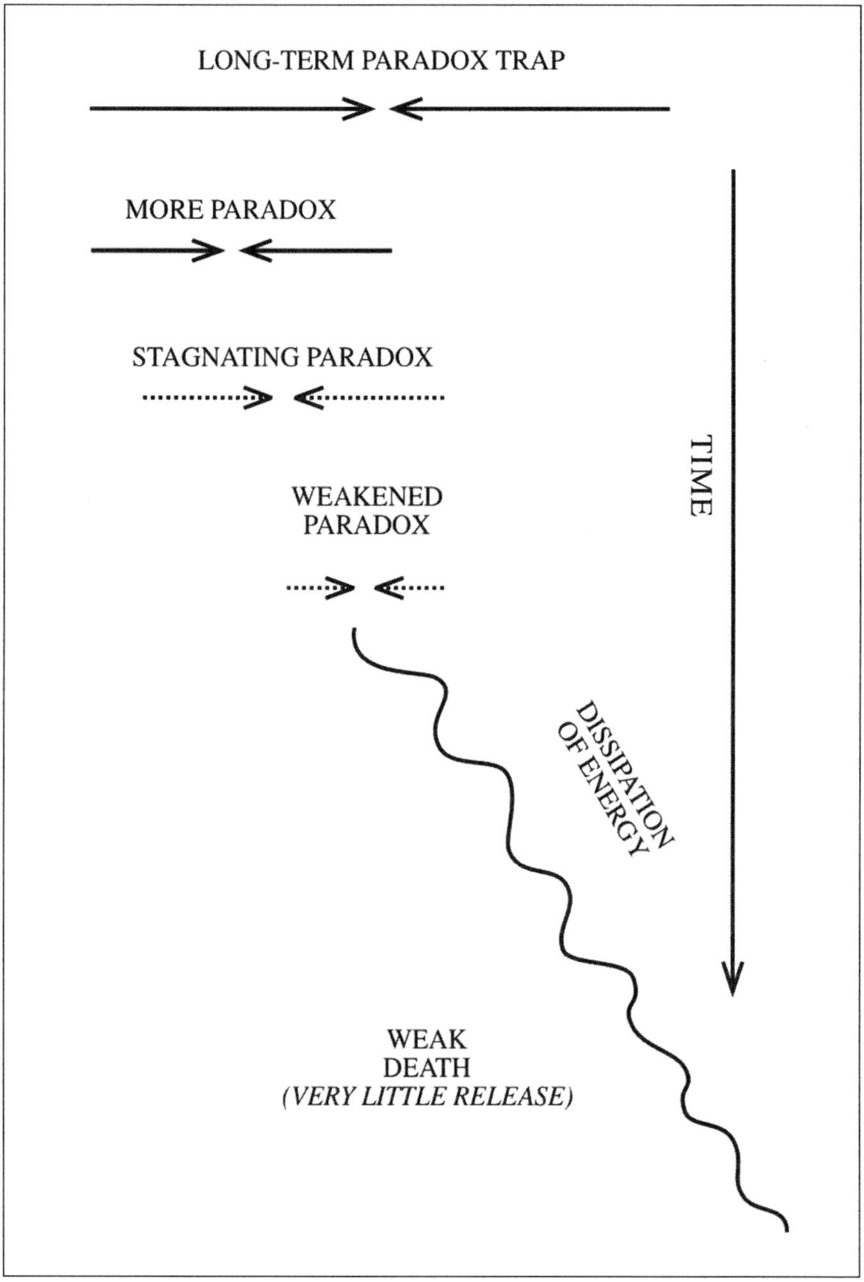

Figure 6.4. Death map three: weak death with little release.

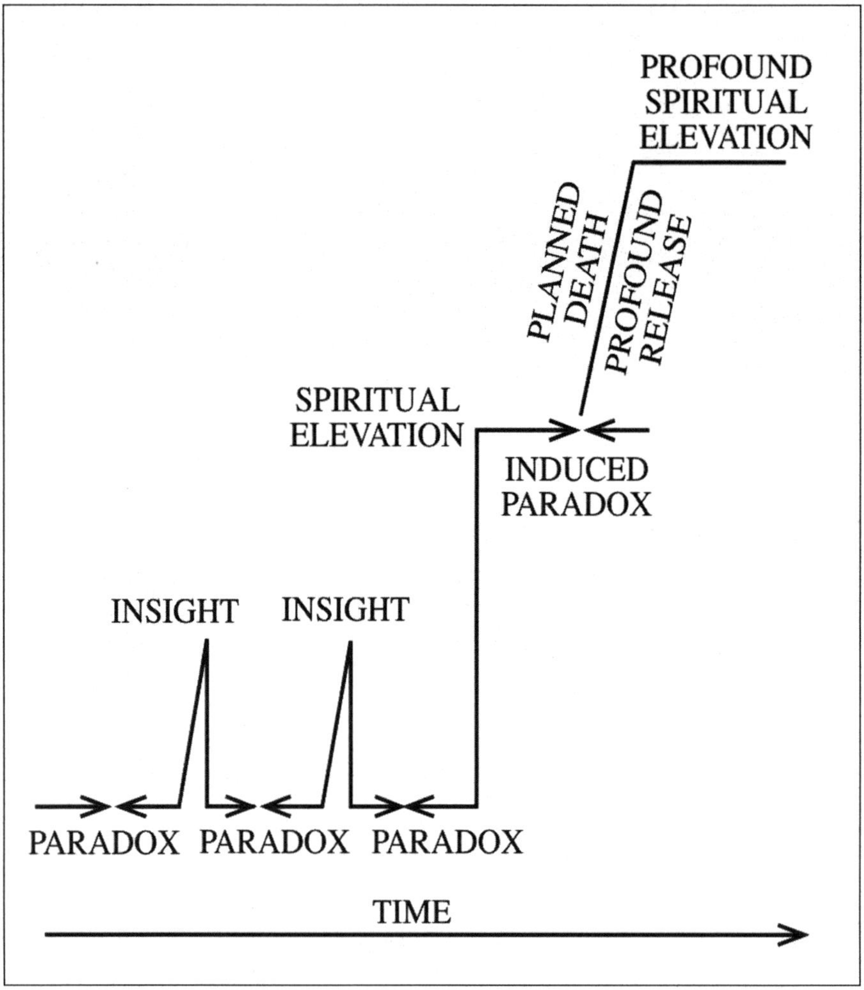

Figure 6.5. Death map four: conscious death release.

Chapter 7

Master Transition from One Reality to Another

This chapter formulates transition and death as the shifting of shape, form and self—to and from dimensions of reality, to and from realities—using a metaphorical description of this experience to present key information.

This little book asks you to take in and pull together ancient and modern teachings. Some of this material is a rethinking of medicine and psychology; some of it is a slightly different perspective on politics. Other parts come from what is called esoteric teaching.

Esoteric teaching is defined as teachings that were (or are being) created by powers in religious, political or intellectual organizations or groups. These teachings were (or are) reserved for the select few: the "eso," or inner circle. Esoteric is considered the opposite of "exoteric," exoteric teachings being those teachings that were (or are being) translated for use by the many. These teachings were for the so-called "exo," or outer circle. That abilities and technologies for survival, death and transcendence are still being withheld from the general population is deplorable. This knowledge is every person's birthright.

Why This Esoteric Discussion?

You are being asked to rethink death because you are a far more potent being than most teachers of history, science and religion have told you. You are so expansive a being that your energy field already touches many states of reality, many arrangements of energy, many dimensions. In fact, you are in contact with and living within all dimensions at once, right here. Right here? You might wonder where else you could really be while you are right here!

"Right here" is an elusive concept, even though it sounds concrete. In reality, there is no more of a right here *here* than there is anywhere else. Basically, your sense of location is colored by your ties to physical reality. This physicality is only one dimension of existence. There are many other dimensions or arrangements of energy—those dimensions are already all right here. This is true because you exist—everyone exists—in a matrix of dimensions with varying degrees of physical and nonphysical reality.

Many of you are now asking, "But then, why can't I see these other dimensions?" The answer is that you can see them, but not in the same way you usually see things. You do see time passing (perhaps watching a child grow up) and distance traveled (perhaps on the freeway). And you will see much more when you learn to stop using your physical eyes as the ultimate arbiters of reality, when you retrain your optic nerve and develop your third eye. Everything is right here, whether you can see it or not. Start looking.

The Dimensions of Reality

Everyday life has many faces. Even within the limited realities in which many of us live, there are many realities. Energy is always arranging and rearranging. In every now second, our bodies and our minds are at least slightly different than they were a second ago.

Take some time to think, to let this concept become a part of you—the concept of death as a transition or relocation of energy from one reality to another, from one aspect or dimension of reality to another. Sometimes this transition must travel through several realities or aspects of realities to reach a resting point, the new reality the transition is seeking.

You can make such a transition or relocation of energy with confidence and clarity, whatever the level of transition may be—whether it is a transition out of a relationship, out of a drug addiction, out of an illness or out of a physical body (in the case of biological death). Think of all your changes as simply being shifts from one state of reality to another. The following discussion will help loosen any rigid perceptions of reality that might keep you from knowing this. Allow the ideas to flow into your mentality without working at taking them in. Remember that this discussion is basically telling you that you can learn to consciously rearrange your energy. You can break any energy pattern in which you are trapped.

Use your imagination. You can shrink down or evaporate (your choice) and pass through what feels to the mind to be something like the eye of the needle and then expand right into the relief of what may seem to be space or heaven. You can come and go from that space or heaven—to and from that sort of hyperspace, to and from other dimensions, to and from other vibrational levels of reality—anytime you choose. It is your right to be able to move your self, your mind and your soul around in this way.

This passing through is the way to survive a transition, even a calamitous event (calamity is also a transition, from the time before the calamity, to the time of the calamity, to the time following the calamity). In a passage that may feel like death, you pass right through the so-called eye of the needle and into another dimension of consciousness. In fact, calamity and apocalypse—whether it is an apocalypse that is all in your mind or body, a natural disaster such as an intense earthquake or something even more massive than that—are often reasons for reaching through the eye toward the beyond. The beyond is, simply put, a place where your energy can be free of the detrimental patterns that were trapping it, even if those detrimental patterns were your physical body.

Moving Through the Windows

Everywhere around and within us are opportunities for passages into realities beyond our current patternings. Recall the earlier discussion about how important it is to know when you are at a fork in the road. It is equally important to be able to find these passages—these eye-of-the-needle moments. These windows of opportunity are windows into other realities. They are all around you, but they remain hidden until you train yourself to see them.

With practice, you will find your windows. Yes, they really are windows of opportunity, although they may first appear to be escape hatches, if you can spot them at all. You can move through these windows by imagining yourself or actually becoming what you visualize as being very, very small or compact, or by becoming so very spread out and so vast that you have no physical density. Remember that you can become very dense (becoming a sort of nowhereness) or become spread very thin (becoming a sort of everywhereness). It is your own choice, in any moment that you have available to you, to employ these techniques (or not to). Just imagine yourself into the form you choose. Imagination is quite powerful in this way. Imagination gives your consciousness great flexibility and versatility, and it is the consciousness that lives on.

Dimension-Shifting Is Like Death

Moving from one dimension of reality to another is a type of death. All death, including living death in which there is no physical death, relates to this process. The experience will vary depending on the circumstances and, in some instances, depending on your preparation for it. Certainly the sensation of the mouth filling with cement may be a sensation that comes with the passage of the self into nonphysical reality. Certainly there are other sensations that can accompany moving the self through dimensions, such as euphoria, bliss, floating, unweighting, disorientation, or the sensation of shift or struggle.

For example, you may feel as though you are traveling through sheets of glass, shattering each of them as you move and then being propelled by the force of that shattering still deeper through the glass sheets, which continue to shatter as you proceed. Or you may feel blind or think you cannot see anything. You may feel as if you are suffocating, drowning for a while, as if you are trapped on the bottom of a lake or sea. The suffocation may be intense if you let fear take over, with your lungs feeling compressed to what feels like complete flatness.

If you find yourself amidst such an experience, know this is merely a sensation, merely a passage. Think of the maps of transcendence presented in this book, or your own versions of these. Let time pass. After a while, you may see flat slabs of light fly out of the dark, like pieces of broken glass. Imagine that you become one of those pieces of broken glass. Let yourself shatter. Feel yourself breaking apart from your holding pattern, from your structure. If you feel no relief when you shatter, if you still feel compressed to suffocating flatness, hang in there. Let yourself be flat, but take on a fluidity to your flatness. Sense that you are trapped in the surface of a body of water, the top of the lake or sea. You are accepting your reduction to a two-dimensional form for a while. You are shapeshifting—your consciousness is shifting its form—to make it through the eye of the needle, through your passage.

While you are accepting your reduction to a two-dimensional form, you will remember this description. You will know that the intense flatness, the compression you feel, is merely a passing state (unless you choose to stay in that compressed form). Should you have such an experience, you are indeed passing through the flatness of two-dimensional reality, where everything exists on a plane. But even as this is happening to you, you may cling to your earthly views of reality. You may have no sense that you are compressing in order to launch yourself. In terms of cross-dimensional travel, you can say that you are launching yourself from the third dimension into the second in order to move into the fourth and escape a pattern of danger, of eventual physical (or emotional) catastrophe on the third. You may do this instinctively. However, it is best for you to do this consciously.

If you find yourself in darkness, wait. Remember that a magnificent stream of glistening light will eventually wash through the dark flatness. Ride this light. When you feel air, or something like air, rush into what you think is your lungs, you will realize with relief that you are not really dead. Instead of dying, you have just traveled across dimensions. You have just crossed one or more thresholds.

Time or Dimensional Travel

You become a reflection, just a flat reflection of your three-dimensional self. Becoming flat, two-dimensional, is one way to bounce into the fourth dimension. In the fourth dimension, where time travel is the typical form of motion, one way to travel around town or around the planet is to shrink, then expand.

The third dimension, the material plane, is located toward what we can call (from our material-plane perspective) the middle of all the dimensions of reality. If you want to move up a dimension, to move around in time either backward or forward, you may first have to move your energy down a dimension (as described below). If you learn to do this well, you may be able to return from this springboard—from this time-dimension shift or time travel—back to the third dimension with your body intact and even with the clothes you had on when you left, if you choose to.

You can alter your physical condition by working on your energy arrangements while in a higher, less physical dimension. Later, if you choose to become more dense, more physical, you will be changed. This raising of one's energy to a higher frequency, to a less dense form, allows for rearrangements, restructurings and healings (what are, in essence, deaths) that can then be moved by the consciousness back down to the physical plane.

Know the Dimensions of Energy

As you master the use of your energy and raise the power of your consciousness, you will have more ability to navigate all your deaths and transitions. Mastering the dying process—or transitional passage—makes life very worth living. In fact, only when death is mastered is life lived. To master death, you must know the dimensions. Basically, the dimensions are a rainbow of realities, with the most-dense reality at one end and the least-dense at the other. First, there is the dimensionless point, the zero dimension:

And a point, when extended, forms a line, a row of points:

This line represents the first dimension, because it has only one dimension—length. When you drag that line, you get a row of lines, or a plane:

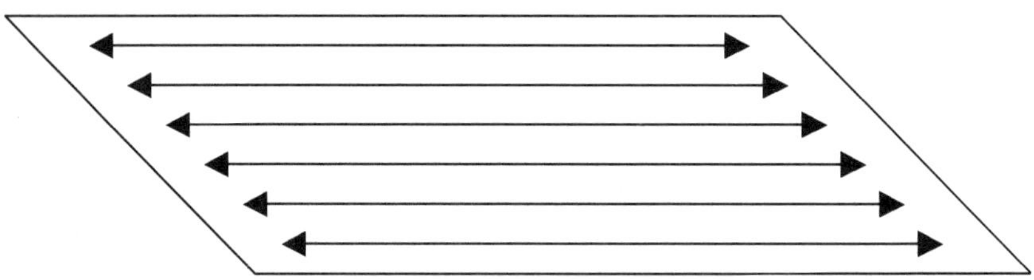

This is the second dimension, because it has only two dimensions: length and width. When you drag this plane through space, you get something with depth. Now the length and width of the plane also have depth, the way a cube does. This is thus three-dimensional reality, which you know well:

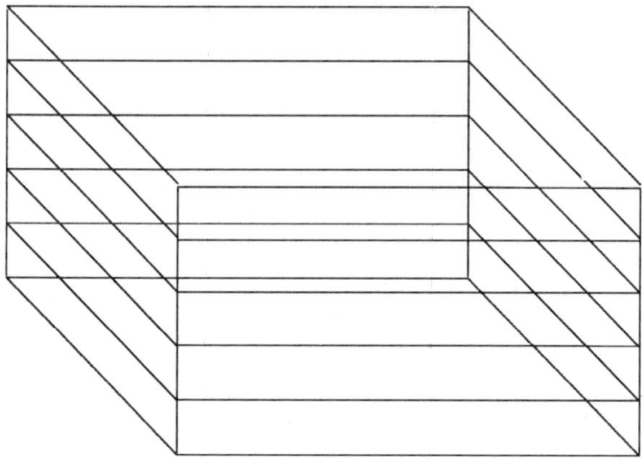

Living in a physical body, one that ages over time, you physically exist primarily on the border of the third and fourth dimensions. Any three-dimensional life form moving through time is, to some degree, traveling in the fourth dimension. But the agility of that life form's travel is a bit hampered by its ties to third-dimensional structure, the physical body in which it lives, as is diagrammed in Figure 7.1.

Of course, if you move that physical form rapidly enough, faster than the speed of light for example, it transforms into something far less dense. Here let's just say that the sides come off of the cube as the cube transforms into something else [see Figure 7.2], into a new form, a new and more nonphysical matrix—even if we cannot see the logic of the new form from where we sit.

The dimensions above your material dimension of reality progress geometrically, just as do the point, the line, the plane and the three-dimensional object. But it is difficult for many of us to see the progression beyond the dimension or condition of reality we think we know best, which here tends to be three-dimensional reality.

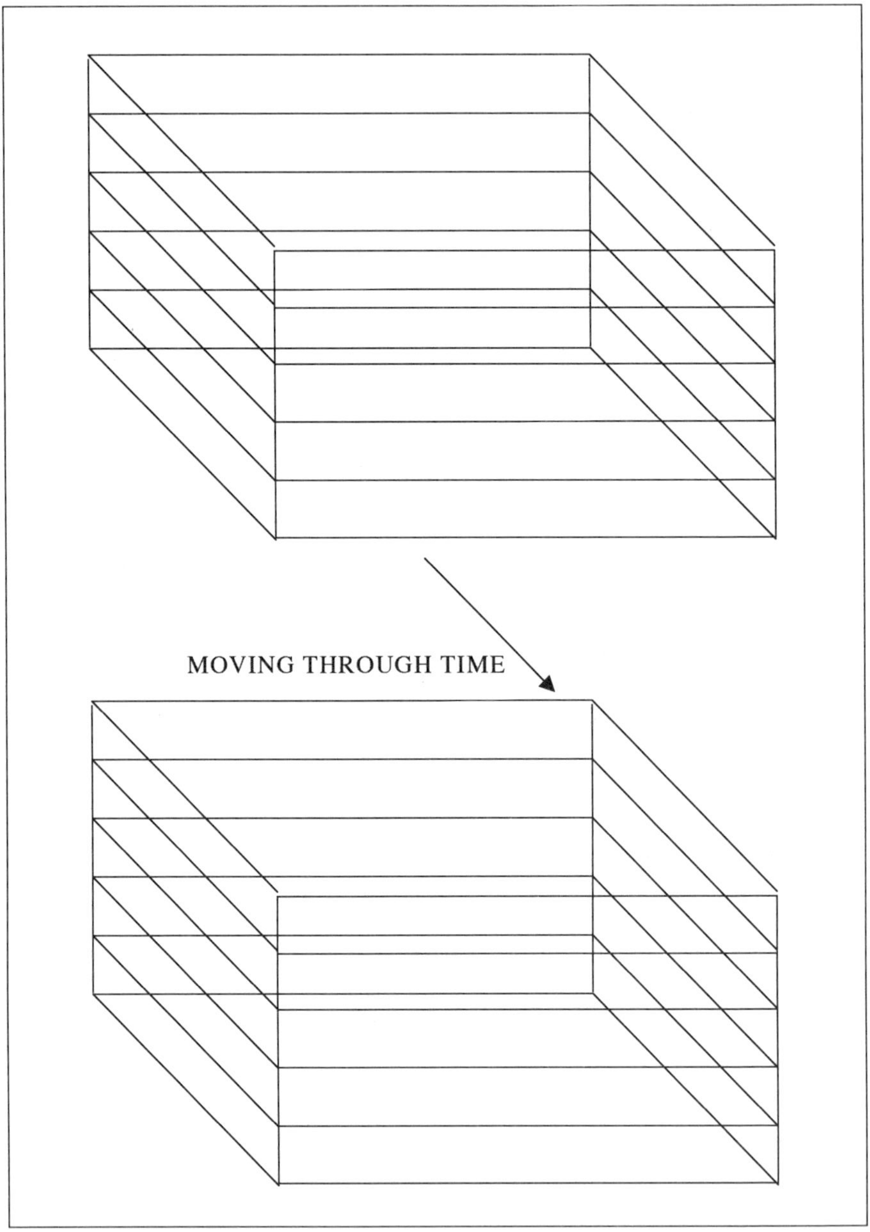

Figure 7.1. A cube moving through time.

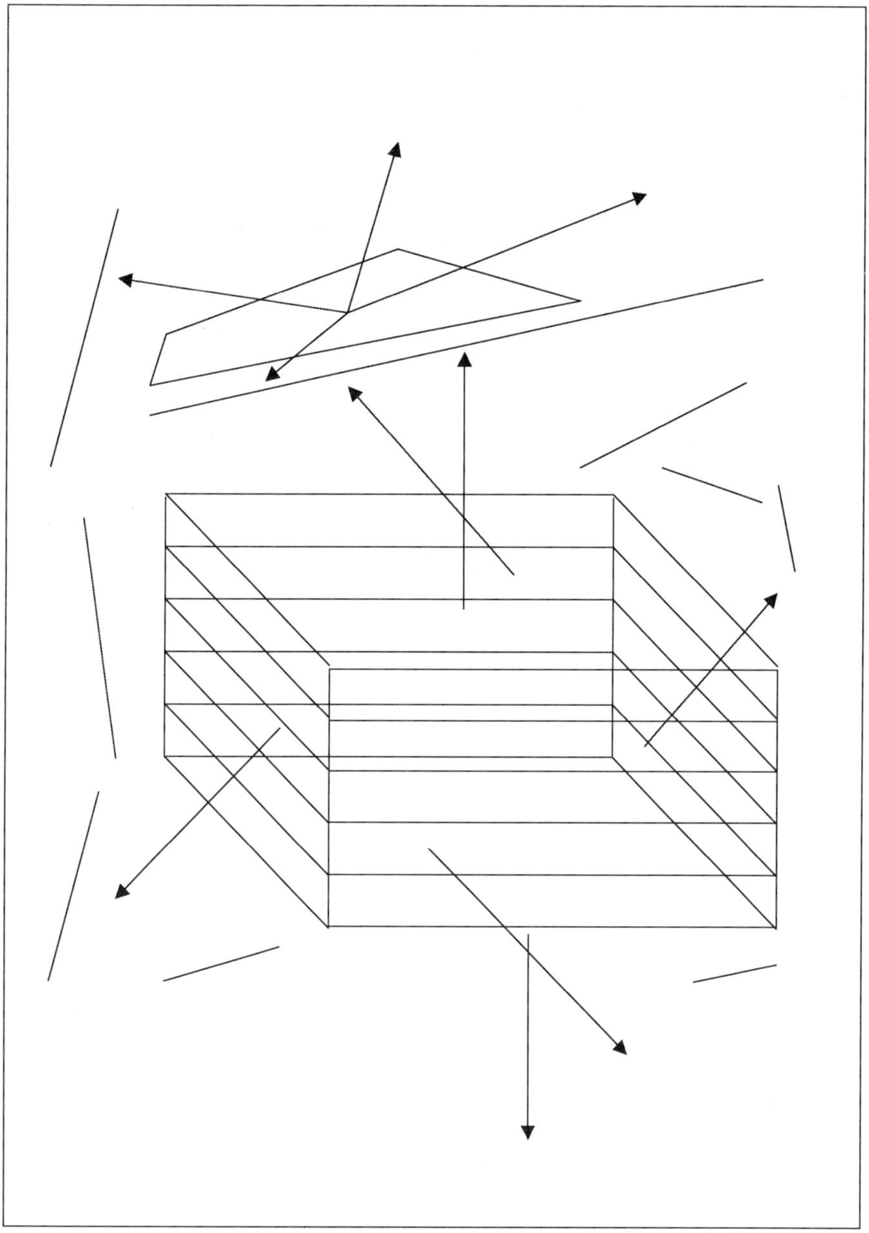

Figure 7.2. A cube moving through time, physically unforming and expanding.

Introducing LEAP Technology

Move the three-dimensional object (the cube) through time with its length, width and depth each moving through time in its own direction, and you have an incredible expansion. This is the time burst typical of the full fourth-dimensional energy expansion. This time burst signifies what we can call the leap into the fourth dimension. A leap is a movement from one dimension to the next, one that is usually best and most efficiently brought about when consciously constructed. This leap is, of course, a death, as each shift in dimension or reality is a form of transition or death. The more trained the dying being is, the cleaner the death leap. This leap, the death leap, is actually something that takes place on many levels. This leap is the light-energy-action process (LEAP) more fully described in later volumes.

L = light

E = energy

A = action

P = process

Now take that energy expansion and raise it yet another level. Do not think about this too hard. Just let your mind review the nature of the mental or experiential shift needed to go from the idea of a point to the idea of a line or a straight piece of thread; from the idea of a line to the idea of a plane or a flat piece of paper; from the idea of a plane to the idea of a cube or any object; from the idea of an object to the idea of that object or body aging, expanding or bursting out in all directions in a rapid evaporation of its physical self.

Now, with the understanding of the mental shift it takes to think about the movement from one dimension of geometry to another, you can begin to fathom a much higher dimension. Take that burst and evaporating essence and move it to a place beyond motion as you know it, where everything is present and abundant at every moment, where light streams look like slow rivers beneath you. This is the wondrous fifth dimension. Here you can see light moving in and out of time, forming and unforming, appearing and disappearing, slowing down and speeding up, moving in and out of lower dimensions. These light waves are rivers of energy running through realities. You can learn to ride them, again allowing your imagination to teach you.

The physical death process can cast a person unaware into this fifth dimension. To stay conscious and navigate your journey for yourself, divorce yourself from any overwhelming amazement at the beauty you find there. If and when you see entire gigantic galaxies and tiny subatomic particles all at the same time, unaided by telescope or microscope, stay focused on your self. The surprise of such perception tends to dissolve many spirits. If you choose to dissolve at this point, make this a clear and conscious choice. You will be aware that you have no physical body, but you will nevertheless feel your life force and any excitations of it. The divine exhilaration, the ecstasy you will feel, is like being wildly in love but millions of times more intensely. If you do stay conscious here and choose not to dissolve, you will feel with absolute certainty that you are here. You will take the form of a massive but mass-less body of energy.

If and when you dissolve, you will move from this ecstatic fifth dimension to the omnipresent, all-knowing, all-being, everywhere sixth. This is the oneness. Only if you consciously enter the oneness, the sixth dimension, can you return from it at will. The oneness is the unveiled, always present, very clear awareness that you are connected to all that exists throughout the cosmos. When you enter the sixth dimension, you will hear, feel and resonate with a universal throbbing. This is the heartbeat of the cosmos, the all. With this as the outcome, physical death, even an unconscious one, is not potentially miserable (as some fear it to be). Instead, death is a great adventure.

Discerning When Traveling Beyond

There are, however, a few things to watch out for as you enter the oneness. First, there are trick windows, pockets and soul traps that look and feel like the oneness but are not. Only the most sentient and most conscious souls can detect and avoid these deceptive windows and navigate the way out should such a trap be entered. Those who enter such a trap may be reborn into a genetically programmed, pattern-addiction-bound life form who uses its energy, unbeknownst to itself, in service to a cosmic hierarchy of energy domination. Stay aware to stay free.

Stay aware right through all of your dyings. If you realize that you have been enslaved as a pattern-addicted life form, a self-programming entity—then free yourself! Find a death, a living death, through which to do this. Physical shedding without proper training (training that requires much study to absorb) does not provide you the opportunity to master the deprogramming of the self, and this mastery each and every one of us needs. Of course, cycling back into something close to the biological form you left is not all that bad. In fact, this life on Earth is a fabulous learning process. Just know the choices and gain mastery over the decision.

Chapter 8

Shed the Skin

This chapter invites an appreciation of transition and transformation, as well as the transcendence these can bring as natural parts of life. In fact, life can be far richer when consciously undergoing these transitional elevations in consciousness.

Each and every one of us reaches a point in life, usually several times, when our particular reality—our particular way of seeing the world, of behaving, of relating, of being—no longer fits us. That we change over time is not surprising. But we do tend to miss many of the very precious steps within our own transitions. We see baby steps, even celebrate these, in very young children, but less so in ourselves. In reality, we are perpetually in transition. We are always ending and beginning, cycling, spiraling, traveling through hidden as well as visible change. The continuum of change and transition we live on stretches far past the limits we tend to impose upon it, far past biological birth and death.

All Deaths Are a Shedding

Not to be blasé about it, but we might want to think in terms of living through many, many deaths, no single one being more critical than another. This is not to deny the immensely profound nature of physical death, but rather to alert us to the also very important qualities of all deaths, endings and transitions that we undergo. All deaths prepare us for future deaths, future endings and future beginnings. All deaths prepare us for the journeys we are truly on. After all, all deaths are a shedding of old programs and mindsets.

We can be attuned to the need for and/or approach of these sheddings. These are windows of opportunity! We have talked about the importance of being perceptive enough to spot windows of opportunity and, even before that, of being sensitive enough to know when we are at a fork in the road while on our path. Usually, prior to coming to such a fork or window is the arrival at a need for shedding. It works something like the image shown in Figure 8.1.

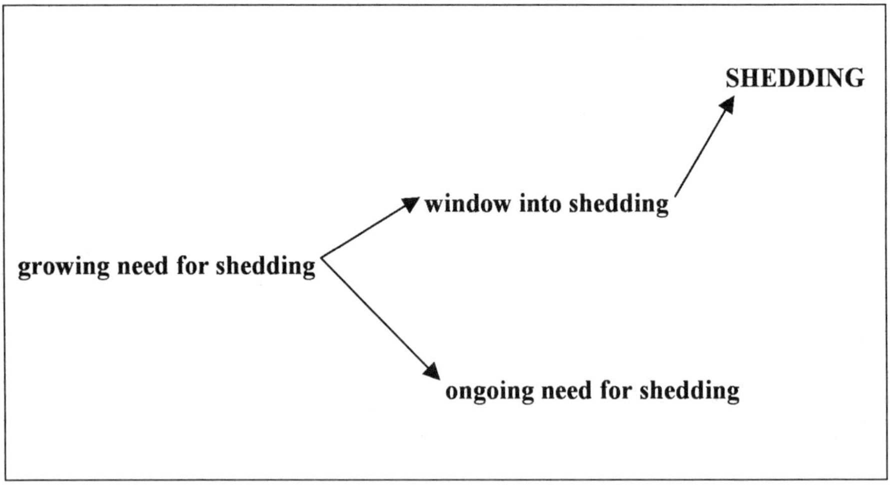

Figure 8.1. The process of shedding.

As with detecting forks and windows, we too often miss seeing that we need to shed our skins and that we are facing opportunities to do so. Of course, sometimes we miss understanding which skin we need to shed and nevertheless feel driven to shed something. This may result in a shedding of the wrong thing. Paying attention when facing this sensation of a need to shed is therefore essential. Far too often we divorce ourselves from the wrong realities. Actually, we can easily miss those signs—we can even miss the fact that we are undergoing our sheddings, not realizing that they are taking place, until we are either deep into the process, completed with the process or well into a much later shedding. Or we miss our sheddings entirely, again not realizing that they have taken place, which results in our not using them well or not bringing them to completion. Stumbling through life and its transitions unaware is a much less effective way to walk.

Whether or not we see our sheddings, shedding is as much a part of life and death as any other function. You shed skin cells and hair every day. In cycles of every seven or so years, you recycle every cell in your body. If you are an adult, you have most likely already shed several relationships and behaviors. There is no point in your physical life when you are not shedding something. Shedding makes room for the new. People who die physical deaths shed their bodies. Basically, most of our physical deaths take place when we have outgrown, worn out or damaged our bodies. Upon physical death, our bodies are then no longer the vehicles we inhabit, no longer the vehicles for the particular journey we have acquired and grown these physical bodies in order to complete.

The same is true of our relationships, our jobs, our addictions and many of our behaviors. There always comes a time for the shedding of these. Some sheddings may appear to be complete cut-offs, endings or abrupt deaths. Others may be recognized for what sheddings are—transitions, transformations and transcendences of the patterns within behaviors or relationships.

Know Momentum

If you have ever been driving a quickly moving car and had to stop abruptly, you have experienced the forward motion of the body and its energy. You know that your body energy continues to move forward in space and time even after the car has stopped. Similarly, in a more expanded and infinite way, physical death offers a parallel: a much more long-lived extension of momentum. The physical body may stop; it may be shed, but the life force does not have to die.

Your life force has a momentum, a character that is registered far beyond the physical realm. In fact, life force cannot be measured in third-dimensional ways. Life force is so immense and so expansive that there are no finite methods in finite realities for gauging this force. Meet your life force, get to know your life force and understand that you can communicate with your life force and direct it where you choose to have it go in life and in death—in all deaths. Commit to knowing that your life force does not have to die.

How to Know That Your Skin Is Too Tight

Again, too often the pressure to shed sneaks up on us without our understanding what it means. We finally notice that the skin of a relationship, a behavior or a life is far too tight—that we have outgrown it the way a snake outgrows its skin. Noticing this may involve sensing some things, being told something, feeling pain or getting sick. You will do what it takes to make your conscious self notice.

You can most definitely get more out of the shedding process by recognizing that you are at its threshold. How do you do this? Become very alert to subtleties such as these: Notice shifts in your ability to concentrate. Notice changes in your enthusiasm. Notice when you feel claustrophobic or trapped—physically, emotionally, intellectually, spiritually. Notice that you may have to work to understand what is leading you to feel trapped. Notice if you are regularly exhibiting troubled behavior that is detrimental to yourself or others. Notice to what degree you function on automatic—mindlessly. Notice how you respond when you stop for a moment's reflection and ask yourself, "Who am I, and why am I here?"

If you find that your life takes on less and less meaning for you, pay attention. Do not assume that mere physical survival has meaning. It may and it may not, depending upon the effect that achieving this survival has upon your soul. Is this struggle for physical survival building strong pattern addictions into your nervous system and mentality? You are not your pattern addictions; however, you are at risk of being controlled by them if you do not call them to your own conscious attention.

Signs That You May Need to Shed Something

- **changes in concentration**
- **changes in enthusiasm**
- **claustrophobia or a sense of being trapped**
- **troubled behavior toward self and/or others**
- **automatic or mindless functioning**

You know when it is time to shed your skin. You can let yourself notice when you are feeling caged in, boxed in or trapped by rigid physical, mental, emotional and behavioral patterns that are ruling your life. As you are losing your self and your free will in these traps, you must notice them and screen yourself for them before you are too far gone to do so.

Getting Out

Once you allow yourself to see the truth, to detect the need for shedding, you must let yourself out of your skin. Get out. Here's where there is sometimes strong resistance. Either you or the people around you do not want you to change.

Do not let anyone tell you that you cannot get there from here. This statement reveals our deep programming to accept and to believe in severe limitations. You can get anywhere you want from here. You just need a map and a vehicle. Take steps to plan the death of the body or behavior you have outgrown. Open your eyes to the forks and the windows—they are everywhere! Know when to get out.

Why Some Prefer Physical Death

When you are without the map and the vehicle, or have not yet found the courage to read the map and drive the vehicle, you stay quite stuck. You know the feeling: It's that phase called "paradox" described earlier. Some people remain entirely or substantially within a paradox—the same, repeating or similar sort of paradox—for most of their lives. When the pressure to shed becomes unbearably great, they either get sick and die, or commit suicide and die.

While these are unfortunate, traumatic and sad developments, they are, ironically, when stumbled into unintentionally, easy ways out. Do not misunderstand this comment. Not all physical illness, terminal disease or suicide is the result of a long-term personal resistance to the shedding of paradox. A significant portion of illness and even suicide is the expression of overarching global conditions that are too large for those who are untrained to see. Individuals can manifest population problems. We certainly cannot hold any single individual responsible for larger systemic and population conditions. Yet we as individuals must learn to manage the influence of the system and of the population upon us, to survive this influence and to change this influence. We must realize that our healings and our conscious dyings contribute to this change.

Still, some people are trapped in their personal patterns for a long, long time and remain resistant to dying a living death of the pattern that traps them. They see no exit and no way to shed their skins except through physical death. And then, on some deep cellular level, they decide to get out in this way. Because the decision is usually an unconscious one, it does not appear to be a decision. Instead it is seen as an unfortunate event.

One of the most unfortunate developments is the moving of a troubled behavior pattern from the psychological to the physical realm. This allows trapped energy to become more dense, more physical. It is not surprising that many psychological and spiritual disturbances take on a physical aspect such as drug addiction, sex addiction, domestic violence, accident-proneness and, of course, physical pain and illness. Beings who live in the material plane, as you do, tend to want to pull whatever they can into a place where they can physically see it. There is a drive to "make real" energies that are perceived but not seen.

This drive to physicalize patterns is valuable when it calls attention to energy disturbances and implicit pattern addictions that might not otherwise be seen. Yet at the same time, this "physicalizing" or "somaticization" of a hidden condition can result in physical suffering without any healing or even any recognition of the condition from which it stems. Basically, you can make yourself sick pulling energy into physical form unless you are trained to work with it.

It is best to destructure detrimental patterns before they become physical. This means that one must be highly conscious of these patterns long before they make themselves visible to the physical eye. Much more is accomplished when the work is done above the level of the physical body and plane. Surgery on energy patterns is possible and essential.

The Right to Know the Art and Science of Dying

Physical death can be a great teacher and releaser. This is not intended to advocate for unconscious stumbling into terminal disease or impulsive or irresponsible suicide. However, this is also not an argument against conscious physical death as a respectable way out of the skin of a life that one has outgrown. The right to die must be defended. The art and science of dying must be taught.

We know much more about self-deliverance than we realize. Certainly, there are persons who give advice regarding medicinal and mechanical means of dying. However, there are many ways of detaching from the body that require no assistance. You have a right to this information, but only with the moral commitment to use it wisely.

Chapter 9

Harvest Death

This chapter emphasizes the vast amount of energy released in transitions and dying of all sorts. This energy can be harnessed to propel an elevation to a new level of being, a new level of awareness, a heightened level of spiritual elevation. Once you begin to appreciate the concepts that your major transitions are all deaths and that you can map and master each and every one of your death processes, you begin to gain power over the course of your life and your evolution. As you grow in this understanding, you gain an increasing say in the use of your energy.

You can access the energy flowing through you and through any dimension of reality at any moment you choose. This is free energy. You help manufacture it. You release it into reality. You have as much right to this energy as does anyone or anything else.

Death Is a Gift

Do not fear change. Fear congests and weakens your energy. Remember that throughout the cosmos there is a perpetual flow of change in which forces are always interweaving and disentangling, contracting and expanding. This is called *samsura*, or "incessant motion," by Buddhists. Some of the motion is smooth and some of it is convulsive, but all of it is change. Change is incessant. And so when a change feels in any way like a death, see it as a gift. Change is, after all, the freeing of energy from the chains of patterns that are binding it.

Resistance to change means that you risk stagnation. Being trapped for a long time or experiencing a long-term paradox becomes a stagnation of energy. Too many elect of their own free will (or what they believe to be their own free will) to stagnate, to go against the flow, to resist change. This is not surprising. We have not allowed ourselves and have not been allowed by others to fully understand the dynamics of change. We are held in an unenlightened state because we are more easily controlled in such a state—controlled by our own pattern addictions, our own political systems and likely by other invisible forces too large for us to see.

The unenlightened resist change, seeing it as threatening, seeing death as the end rather than as a shift into a new dimension of reality. The enlightened person does not resist the flow of the life force throughout the dimensions but opens to a recognition of this flow and a movement with this flow. The greater your understanding of this dynamic order, the more your actions will harmonize with it.

Of course, harmonizing takes real attention so as not to be pulled in the direction of false harmonies, illusions of harmonies and energy predators who may present invitation into pseudoharmony as bait. A greater and more conscious understanding of harmonization can prevent the kidnapping of your energy. Just as there are predators in the jungle, there are forces in all dimensions that seek to use your energy arrangements, transitions and releases for their own purposes.

Individual and Species Energy Flow

We have touched on the notion that your energy is yours. In that this energy both flows through you and is fueled by you, this energy is indeed yours at the time when it is within you. Because you produce your arrangement of it and you release your arrangement of it, you are responsible for what it does and where it goes during the time when this energy flows from you. This means that you as a responsible being must learn to master the flow of your energy in and out of life transitions and dimensions of reality.

You must be as conscious as possible of the phases of transition and transcendence. You must be alert for indications of sheddings, forks and windows. You must stay conscious through all your deaths—physical and nonphysical—in order to be certain you do not inadvertently surrender, sign over or land your energy in a place where you lose free will over its use. It is your responsibility, then, to prepare for the appropriate and conscious harvesting of your energy, which takes place during and following each and every one of your dying processes. As individuals increasingly accept this responsibility, we increase the ability of our entire species to do the same.

Prepare for the Harvest

To best prepare for your harvest of your energy, take conscious control of your life's processes and transitions. Although you cannot control all the events around you, you can direct and navigate your ride through them. Become sensitive to the phases, sheddings, forks and windows we have discussed. Notice the energy that is available to you to harvest your transition. Ride the energy through your transition. During difficult transitions, stay focused on a high point within what you feel is your physical body, or focus on a metaphor for the physical body. It is best to select either the area in what you imagine to be the center of the forehead or the top of the head to stay connected to. Hold on to this connection; keep returning to the idea of it, as if there were a cord attached to it. If you want to let go of this cord, you may, but do so quite consciously, as if you are knowingly releasing the reigns while riding a wild horse.

Check the terrain out beforehand. Are there any traps or trick windows leading to dead ends or undesirable nested loops, seeming no-escape repeat pathways for your energy? Can you see clearly what is calling you and coming at you? There are various cord releases that you might undertake at this juncture, but for now, letting go yet being conscious as you do is enough of a description.

Should you elect this form of release, do so knowing that you are freeing your energy for absorption by your environment in time, in space and in the cosmos. The harvest of your life force will no longer be specifically yours. To turn over your harvest, the release of energy brought about by your dying process, is not a detrimental choice, so long as you know well where you are sending it. No matter how challenging the turning-over phase, this release can be most exalting. No matter how rough your ride, how tortured your dying process, it is your responsibility to keep your eyes and all your sensory mechanisms open, and notice what systems are there to receive your energy.

Whether you are dying a death of a behavior or dying a physical death, you must take responsibility for the energy you release when old patterns die. The harvest is yours. Stay conscious of this. Do not sell your product—the arrangement of energy you have cultivated—at the market, unless the exchange is toward an ever-more right use and freedom of that energy. If you feel unprepared to make such an assessment, keep your energy under your wing and continue to evolve it.

Cosmic Democracy

Democracy is practiced here. This is the free and equal right of every one of us to participate consciously in the system of energy evolution and energy transmission across the dimensions, in living and dying, in dying and surviving. Well beyond the bounds of any nation's definition of itself as a democracy is this cosmic aspect of freedom.

Chapter 10

Ride Personal Apocalypse into Power

This chapter characterizes personal travails as events along a path to increased understanding and consciousness power. The path of any dying process can be traveled into a new level of being.

As a human in a physical human body, you know something of the ordeals faced by life forms living in the third dimension. When understood, these ordeals can encourage spiritual growth, increased freedom of will and new power over patterns and illusions that otherwise trap us. The journey through your human incarnation is superbly challenging, and the potential for what is called "the quickening of the soul" is profoundly immense during your human incarnation. Try to remember this in your living moments of even the most mortal anguish, and try to receive this message in its entirety at the hour of your physical death.

The Denial of More

As a human living in this physical dimension of reality, it is very easy to think nothing exists outside of this third dimension—that there is only material reality and nothing else, and therefore, that all life forms have physical bodies. Although a human often begins to feel that there might be more to her or his reality than meets the physical eye, the assumption that nothing living can really exist without a three-dimensional body often persists.

As the spiritual awareness of a human being matures and evolves, the development of higher, less physical domains of the self takes place. As a life form extends its awareness of reality to beyond the base physical realm, that being becomes less and less physical, less and less dense (in an average density-across-time-and-space sense), and more and more aware of its expansion into realms less physically dense than its physical body. Try to encourage this trend in yourself. You will be contributing to your own and your species' evolution.

The full essence of the universe is one that likely lies beyond the grasp of the existing human intellect. Fortunately, the collective human mind is beginning to progress through the development of its intellect into a new form of intelligence, one that may someday be an active intelligence, a highly conscious metacognitive intelligence.

The Importance of Density

An understanding of density is essential here, both to ease the passage from physical death to the beyond and, while in this particular lifetime, to understand how programming and pattern addiction can be transcended. In reading the following, remember that it helps to think in pictures in order to make an understanding of density work for you. You are, in a sense, being asked to lighten up, to de-densify. In a less dense form, your energy is more expansive, more malleable and more easily rearranged. Attempt to see the light described below as a river of energy.

The less dense and the more like fluid light that you allow yourself to become, the greater your awareness will grow. Fluid light is not very dense; it has almost no density. Beings, life forms, take on varying degrees of density. A life form locates itself along a continuum of most dense to least dense, least light to most room for light. Within each dimension, the least-dense life forms are the most evolved. As you grow in consciousness, your awareness and your mentality become less dense. This can feel "ungrounding" to those unschooled in this process. By inching your awareness up the scale of decreasing density, your mind and your soul become less weighed down by the compactness of belief in physical reality as the *only* reality.

As this "unweighting" takes place, the actual diminishing of your body relative to the expansion of your energy begins. You may feel somewhat crazed by this sensation, as if you are "losing it" or "coming unglued." If so, you are experiencing the unsettling effects of de-cohesion, diminishing cohesion. You are really feeling the effect of enhanced entropy. Entropy is the tendency of matter to dissipate in the process of de-cohesion. As matter becomes less dense, less compact and less cohesive, it gains entropy and dissipates increasingly. It weighs less and less per cubic millimeter and is thus less weighed down. The physical matter of you becomes less tightly organized in a material sense but more complex in a multidimensional sense.

Try not to think about this too much. One of the dangers of overintellectualizing important concepts is that it can cause a misunderstanding of reality. Just allow these ideas to be with you. Think in pictures or in diagrams if it helps. After a while, these ideas will be absorbed and will thus become comprehensible. The most-dense life forms are found in the lower dimensions, where essences are most compact. The least-dense life forms are found in the higher dimensions of reality. Understand that compactness and density accompany each other. Density blocks light, and light is needed to navigate transition. Density is a state of mind, as is lack of light.

Consciousness Technology

Awaken your consciousnesses. Learning to move your being through density is essential. To do so, you must become increasingly adept in consciousness technology. This is the technology by which consciousness can become highly aware of itself and profoundly enhance its functioning and freedom.

You are definitely able to manifest your essence in increasing complexity and vastness throughout all the dimensions. You, just as any life form, can evolve increasing degrees of consciousness. You are already part of a life system of conscious interaction—a social system that has a government and an economy. But how much freedom is available to you within the system you belong to? A higher level of consciousness must be achieved in order to transcend the lower systems and patterns in which we live and to preserve free will.

Reaching Through to the Supermind

This means that you must learn to recognize the "supermind." Untrained, your efforts may not reach you through to the supermind. Your ignorance may not manage to transcend itself. So how do you, with physical-reality limitations, ascend to your rightful place in the cosmic hierarchy of energy? Your ascendance can be actuated by the consciousness force, which works toward the emergence of its powers into each being's—in this case, *your*—consciousness. You can allow this superconscience to descend into you and uplift you, to formulate the process of your transcendence and ascendance back to your rightful level of high consciousness. However, you must wait until you have studied the surrounding subtle realities enough to know when you are in contact with the true superconscience and not a force posing as the superconscience. Otherwise, you are surrendering your energy to a higher power, but not necessarily the higher power you would choose of your own free will had you enough information to do so.

This concept is important, in that during the dying process, whether it is a living transition or a physical shedding, energy is released. As noted elsewhere in this book, this energy is sometimes released to other than one's own consciousness. For example, many persons recovering from explicit addictions are overwhelmed by their newly released energy and quickly give it away again. Sometimes they trap it in the same or a new pattern addiction; sometimes they surrender the energy to someone or something else that will control it. You can evolve without outside intervention, even without superconscience assistance. The elements of the higher consciousness you seek are already present within you. Accessing these and developing them is the challenge. Decide for yourself, but decide consciously and stay conscious. The journey is yours. Travel it your way.

Believing in More and Finding It

Most life forms see so little of what is really here. Life forms define their realities based upon the illusions they allow themselves to believe in. All they really see are shadows of truth and shadows of reality. In these shadows live the illusions that hold us captive. Turn on the light! Death is not what you may believe it to be. Nothing dies in the so-called conventional sense, because nothing stops moving—matter is always in motion, whether organic or inorganic. Examine information for truth. Humans must do this. Truth has been severely distorted by language and culture. The precious consciousness of humanity is buried within an elaborate hierarchy of distortion, which veils truth. Human words and beliefs are too often part of this elaborate distortion.

A spiritual truth, to be honestly relayed in its wholeness, cannot be distorted. A spiritual truth, without ever being intellectualized by the brain of a human or any other life form, can congeal into an experience, an awareness, an image or a symbol. That experience, awareness or image can again unfold in the eye of its beholder—depending upon the sophistication of the beholder, in terms of his or her readiness and willingness to see—into varying degrees of truth. Let this unfolding begin within you. When you are ready to understand the truth, you will recognize it as it comes to you.

Power Is in Knowing Who You Are

Know who you are. Know that every individual soul is a microconsciousness, one that affects the macroconsciousness. Every soul vibrates at its own frequency of consciousness. This frequency can be raised—evolved—by that soul. Spiritual evolution is a constant developing of form, spiritual form. Development involves journeying through all dimensions of reality. The sole purpose of any spirit coming into the third dimension of reality (such as you have on Earth) is to work toward manifesting the indwelling spirit, the spirit you carry within you. When free to, nature evolves in this direction: the progression is from matter toward mind. The evolution of matter through time is from the lower to the higher dimensions. Every soul has the right to ascend to a higher plane and a higher consciousness.

Commit to this growth for the good of us all. Your great soul has the potential to advance the evolution of humanity and of other souls (whether human or not), and to spread true enlightenment. You are a great soul. You can bring the energy generated by a transformation of your own consciousness to the collective energy pool. You can contribute to a global cosmic transformation that will help end the dictatorial cultivation, wasting and kidnapping of your physical-plane energies. Always seek authenticity in the expression of your power—do not be fooled by the temptations of self-doubt and negativity. The fear of authenticity and the nonchalance and noncommitment that accompany this fear can cause you to surrender to the enslavement of denial, lies, untruths, greater pattern addiction and the capturing and killing of free will. You can help to protect free will by becoming free.

Now that we have said that there is no such thing as death, an elaboration on this is necessary. There is a great difference between cyclical and absolute death. When free will disappears entirely from the cosmos, this will be the absolute death of free will. Matter and energy may live on eternally; however, will can be permanently eliminated. This is not an adventure in death—this is the end of the life of the energy force you have come to call freedom. Do not allow this transition into an entirely mechanical, programmed, robotic, will-less, soul-less universe to happen. Stay conscious. Wherever free will is diminished, fuel its return to its fullest potential. Draw upon the life force to feel free will. The life force does not die: Free will is fueled by the life force.

Chapter 11

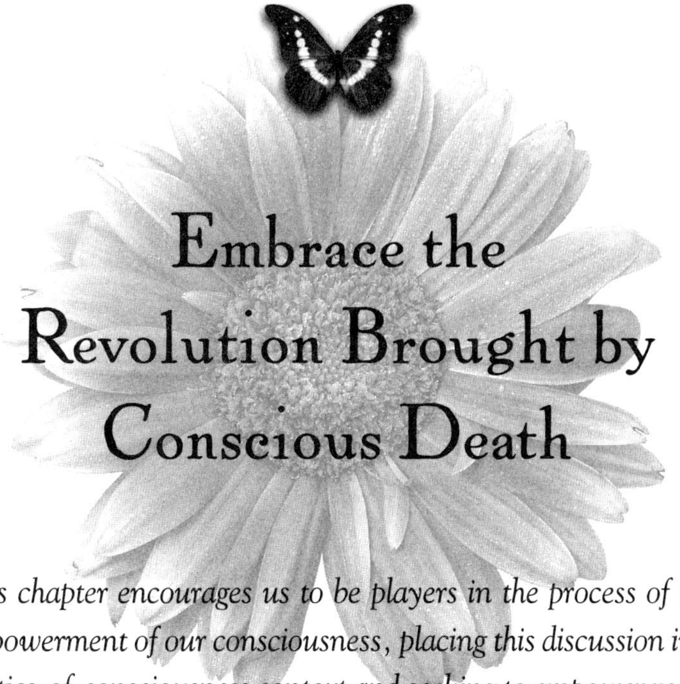

Embrace the Revolution Brought by Conscious Death

This chapter encourages us to be players in the process of the empowerment of our consciousness, placing this discussion in a politics-of-consciousness context and seeking to empower readers to recognize that mastery of life's cycles, of life and death, will contribute to the evolution of human consciousness.

We think; therefore, we are. But who are we? What thinks? The brain? The mind? Is there a difference? And what is "thinking"?

Contained in a skull no larger than a deflated soccer ball and physically manifested in the form of a wrinkled blob we call a brain, the human mind is a cagey, intractable entity—difficult to locate but without boundaries, capable of amazing feats but weak and fallible, seemingly autonomous and yet tending toward the convenience of supposedly survival-oriented preprogramming, which often results in undesirable and sometimes terrible habitual behaviors and other pattern addictions.

One of the toughest of all our pattern addictions is our addiction to our reality. Somehow we allow our dependence on what is—what we think is, our deep reliance on the illusion we call our reality—to be a "reality check" on all reality. We cling to what we think is, refusing to let it die unless we are pushed to the edge and lose control or fitfully relinquish it. And then there is an unnecessarily tortured death, rather than a fruitful one.

When the world as we know it, the reality upon which we have become so dependent, dies, do we die too? Must we die too? No. They say that we live, therefore we die. But who says this? Who lives? What dies? Are we all held prisoner by a lie?

The Politics of Death

Could death be something different from what we have come to believe it is? Can we break free of the shackles of our realities and see through our fears; our suffering; our difficult transitions; our mental, emotional, spiritual and even physical deaths? Can we look through the veil of deception that humans have allowed themselves to live beneath and see truth? Yes! But first we must be willing, must be daring enough to ask ourselves a few questions.

Are we programmed to die? Why do each and every one of our cells have implanted within them a genetic plan to die off after a certain number of divisions? Are we genetically programmed to die physical deaths? Or are we genetically programmed to believe that we have to die and that physical death is final? Is this programmed belief so all-powerful that it controls us, kills us and threatens to make our deaths final?

You see, if we are convinced (even just a little) that there is no life beyond physical death, we fall prey to that illusion of reality. However, this is not our own illusion. We have been brainwashed into acceptance of the lie about dying. What for? What force or intelligence or energy could have focused upon our genetic coding so closely as to create such a limited reality in our minds? You see, life and death is cyclic, revolving over and over and over. To be allowed to only see enough of death to believe that it is the end, is to be deprived of the truth. The illusion of the finality of death is something we must break through, on all levels, to ensure that we have the freedom to travel our deaths consciously. We must dare to ask a few more questions.

Are we anything but biological, fleshy robots? Do we reflect a sallow mechanical light in our eyes, the light of will-lessness, the glow of hypnotization? Have we succumbed to a daze in modern years, or have we always been part of a very large mindlessness? Are we biotech at its finest, or biotech gone wrong? Can we really be free as long as we are subject to the enslavement of inherited and acquired genetic and neurological programming?

If Earth is a fantastic macrocosmic laboratory and we are prisoner-subjects in a massive experiment too large for our human minds to fathom, then our learning the truth can lead to startling discoveries regarding the programming implanted by our captors. We can and must capture control of our will and set it free. Only a revolution in human awareness can free us. But what would this freedom look like? Would it be much different from the way we live and look now?

Breaking Through the Shackles of Our Programming

These are questions more readily asked than answered. Yet we might move toward an inkling of an answer if we reflect upon the degrees of freedom allowed us by biology. Consider the view that we function on genetic and neurological automatic the majority of the time. We fool ourselves into believing that we exercise a great deal of free will. We are in a state of denial about our mechanical, robotic, programmed and programmable nature.

We living things are not only creatures of habit, we are habit addicts. Yes, as has been explained in previous chapters, our ability to biologically (and even genetically) program ourselves for automatic responses is essential for survival. Speedy responses to danger, for example, save lives. If we had to take time to think through each immediately necessary action, we would probably die off. We rely on our automatic behaviors to respond to physical events, such as falling objects, red traffic lights and other situations that demand a quick response. We also may respond automatically to seemingly less-critical physical events or conditions, such as hunger for a snack, a cold draft in the house or a baby's cry. Some pieces of this behavior are genetically inherited and thus are instinct driven, and other pieces are the result of patterning acquired during day-to-day experiences.

So convenient and readily developed is automatic physical behavior that it merges with the nonphysical realms of human interaction and emotion. Public and private feelings and their expressions are often manifestations of psychological and social patterns. It is difficult to discern exactly what proportion of an individual's behavior is attributable to the larger social and cultural environment, and what proportion is particular, idiosyncratic to the individual. We have evolved a population-wide machine that holds us here, locked in this so-called reality, believing in too many of its limitations. These are not our limitations; they do not belong to us. The power of belief is immense, and therefore, belief itself must shift at the deepest levels.

It is certainly difficult to separate the larger social and political behaviors of the human population on Earth from the genetic directive to be addicted to a limited reality dictating false limitations to us. This physical-plane genetic directive is nested within each physical cell within each and every human. Yet we are so much more than physical beings that we need not be controlled by physical programming—or any programming, for that matter.

The Distraction of Consumption

A built-in drive (a program) to consume distracts us from our essences, depriving us of our power. So much of our cultural overlay is dedicated to the selling and feeding of food and drugs to the consumer, and to fueling the ever-present and ever-growing compulsion to buy things, things, things. We are bombarded by advertisements to buy anything and everything, to eat anything and everything, and to drug ourselves with anything and everything. Is overconsumption, driven by addiction to these things, merely an individual malady, or is it a species-acquired response to environmental stimulation that has been created (based upon its programming) to control?

We are so very consumptive, so very driven to consume and so addicted to consuming that we are distracted from who we are and what we truly are. Once a consumption-driven behavior, no matter what its origin, is repeated a number of times, a program is eroded into the neural pathways that have transmitted the biochemical message required to repeat the act. The more repetition, the deeper the erosion and the more automatic the behavior. The robot within us rises, run by automatic biological programming mechanisms. The robot within us is at once the prison and the prisoner of life. Meet the biological robot: you, me, everyone. But robots can rebel!

Death as Erasure of Programming

It has been implied by several scientists that there is no way, except perhaps by physical death, to clear the mind of all past impressions and programming. Those who believe in the spill-over of experience from lifetime to lifetime will claim that even physical death is not a clearing. But let us say, for argument's sake, that physical, biological death is indeed an effective means of erasure, and that only this sort of death offers complete erasure. Biological death, then, is a sure means of overcoming or transcending a problematic personal condition, especially if the problem condition is (as are most conditions of human behavior) subject to neurological and other forms of biological patterning. Physical death, under appropriate circumstances, is an honorable option.

Or maybe physical death is not a complete erasure but instead a sort of amnesia, allowing whatever it is that may live on when the body dies a chance to forget its own biological programming. What a marvelous opportunity this might be for those who are deeply dissatisfied with the programming that they have either inherited or acquired. But we cannot be certain that all deaths guarantee transcendence of programming. It is therefore as important to die well as it is to live well. Preparation for death is preparation for transcendence.

Again, this is not to advocate physical death as the only way out of problem conditions. Too many lives turn around, too many healings and recoveries take place, to believe that there is no way except physical death to escape unpleasant physical health, mental health and lifestyle patterns. Physical death is merely one category of death along a large continuum or matrix of deaths. Physical death is not the only way to heal a troubled pattern. Death, in whatever form it might take, may offer the opportunity for transcendence but in no way guarantees it. Again, it is important to die well, whether or not the death in question is biological. Death can be life-healing when conducted consciously.

Becoming a Spiritual Revolutionary

Programmed people are not free; they are robots proceeding to function as programmed. Whatever bit of the soul nestled within the heart of a pattern-addicted being is trapped, caged and suffocating. Too many spirits allow themselves to be suffocated by patterns, eventually permanently extinguishing themselves. Any master plan of any cosmos that planned for this development can be overthrown now.

This restrictive programming is not our own intelligent design. Too many souls are being enslaved by detrimental programming, turned into robots and lost. The massive stagnation and extinguishing of the free will of human souls threatens the perpetuation of all freedom within all creation. You become a sort of revolutionary when you master death. This is because the limits to your reality, your prison walls, have been broken through by you.

The Politics of Healing

The process of breaking addiction to a destructive pattern is a revolutionary experience for an individual. It also has revolutionary implications for society, because transcending addiction to a reality calls for fundamental changes in the way the addicted person sees the world. For an addicted world to transcend pattern addiction, the human race must see all of reality with new eyes. When people change their worldviews and the behaviors that stem from those said worldviews, they inevitably affect the lives of the people around them. Through this process, every time a pattern addiction is transcended, there are political ramifications. Breaking pattern addictions changes the reality of the species.

There are many, many caring and concerned members of the health care community who are actively seeking to aid their clients and patients in the struggle to transcend addictions and afflictions. But the sad truth is that much of the health care community has become mired in the "traditional" conception of the addicted and of the "medically" afflicted person's path and plight. As a result, the health establishment has become rather comfortable in its misdirected insinuations. Hence, the following messages are incorrect and misguiding, and have therefore here been labeled as wrong:

- **Wrong:** Pattern addictions must be explicit to be read.
- **Wrong:** Only members of the health care establishment can detect and diagnose a health problem.
- **Wrong:** The diagnosis that the health care establishment makes is the only diagnosis possible and the only diagnosis that is correct.
- **Wrong:** Observed symptoms have only certain, predetermined, official diagnoses.
- **Wrong:** The treatment of the symptom called for by a diagnosis is the only correct treatment.

- **Wrong**: All symptoms are exactly the symptoms they appear to be.
- **Wrong**: If the health care establishment does not see the underlying implicit pattern addiction or the source of this, it is not there.
- **Wrong**: When what appears to be the same symptom turns up in two different individuals, both individuals are diagnosable and treatable in the same way.
- **Wrong**: Only those exhibiting the symptoms need treatment.
- **Wrong**: The designated treatment will work.
- **Wrong**: The symptoms will be eased or will disappear when the explicit malady is ameliorated or eliminated.

Think about it. By controlling the diagnostic and treatment processes, the health establishment has a stranglehold on the way we think about addiction and illness. Truly healing has become secondary to maintaining a reality—and, of course, a profit margin based on that reality. Old ideas die hard, especially when loss of dollars is involved. Instead of seeking radical transformation in the definition and diagnosis of mental and physical afflictions, the health establishment unwittingly kills us by perpetuating its diagnostic monopoly. And so we continue to suffer from an information breakdown. Information regarding the true and pervasive nature of pattern addiction does not circulate. It cannot circulate easily.

How would the establishment adopt a revised diagnosis of pattern addiction for most illnesses? For example, in recent decades, it has become painfully obvious that drug addiction is not the problem the health establishment has defined it as being.

Diagnosis has a political component. We should be diagnosing the entire global society, not separate individuals. Until we are willing to face this global diagnosis, we are at war with truth. We are experiencing massive societal denial about chemical dependence and many other explicit addictions, including those to spending, relationships, food and violence. We are also experiencing massive societal denial—species-wide denial—about all underlying pattern addictions in the same way that individual addicts experience denial when they say they are not addicted. The entire species is addicted to its implicit patterns. No one in a biological body is exempt. A person's illness is not an individual condition.

Free Will and the Pattern-Addicted Society

Could it be that in some subtle way our global society is working to keep large numbers of its members dependent on chemicals, behaviors, ways of thinking and other detrimental illusions? Again, we must ask: Are we biotechnology at its finest, or biotechnology gone wrong? And do we really have a say about this?

Think about the implications of your own underlying pattern and source addictions. A little addict-person lurks deep inside you. He lurks deep down in your subconscious, waiting for an opportunity to "drive" you, to commandeer your decision-making processes. You may think that you live free, but you are deluding yourself. You are actually a prisoner of your little addict-person, and he will eventually find and exploit your weaknesses—if he hasn't done so already. How readily we succumb to the subtle but continuous diminishing of human freedom when we trade away personal freedom for pattern addiction.

To relinquish the freedom of responsibility, of self-control, to an automatic reality addiction is, in modern lingo, a cop-out. Rather than cope with reality, you let your little addict-person feed you mechanisms that muffle your consciousness, stifle the stresses of life along with your alertness and offer you the illusion of relief—vacations from the demands of truth. Yet we know the truth will set us free. Eventually, the wonderful and usually subconscious lie of pattern addiction turns sour—but by then, it is too late. You have become a slave to your patterning. Only an internal revolution, a complete overhaul, can set you free again. Transcendence is this revolution, this overhaul.

Understanding what it means to say, "I am addicted to my patterns," is a difficult process. Feeling what it takes to know, "I am an addict," is painful. Acknowledging that you are a reality-addicted individual—because we all are—precipitates a sense of what "ought to be" and creates a pressure to break the cycle of pattern addiction. That "ought to" begins to lurk in the innermost recesses of the self, where the free will and the living soul have retreated.

The expected anguish of exorcising an invader—of ripping out an automatic pattern that has taken you over and become embedded within your own nervous system—seems to make it easier to stay with the addiction than to cut it out of your life. Breaking the unwieldy, intractable habit cycle seems as impossible as turning the tide or halting an avalanche. The myopic and eventually blind security of pattern addiction seems relatively comfortable when you are staring into the face of the harsh reality of personal responsibility and freedom. For the pattern-addicted individual, there is always the fear that reality will hurt more than addiction. Mindless obedience often appears more comfortable than profound change, and pattern slavery appears safer than freedom.

Surrendering to any damaging pattern addiction is a counter-soul experience. Addiction with no release is an ongoing state of struggle and paradox, which eventually causes an individual to undergo soul-death—a false, aspiritual and tragic death in which the loss of self becomes final, succumbing to an absolute unwillingness to break out of a paradox and let detrimental programming die. Progressive addictive behavior is a process of surrender in which the will is eroded until the will of the individual eventually disappears. Independent decision-making capabilities become commandeered by robotic, mechanical tendencies. The human biotechnology rolls over and plays machine, soul-dead.

As free will and self-control erode away, a vacuum of vulnerability is left inside the mind of the pattern-addicted individual. This vacuum sucks in outside agents: chemicals, detrimental forms of relationships to other people and so on. Opportunistic physical diseases, social forces and organizations move in and take control. They take over the decision-making processes that could have been controlled by the free will of the individual. When this happens, we surrender our basic human right to individual power and the realization of our own spirituality, and therefore relinquish our collective humanity.

The truth about the advance of pattern addiction is that it has prepared us to be evermore unwittingly controlled—to not only relinquish our free will, but worse, to forget what free will is. This is the most insidious politic of pattern addiction. We are denying our own freedom when we fail to acknowledge the larger picture. Blind denial is a losing stance. It is time to become conscious and pay attention. It is time to actively ferret out our most damaging implicit as well as explicit pattern addictions, time to seek their actual source. Let our prison walls break down—it is time for us to transcend!

Indeed, we are at a critical juncture in the history of life and time. What you do on Earth while embodied in physical reality (the third dimension) is going to make a great difference. You can contribute to a great and most necessary rebalancing. You can support the fight for free will by beginning with your own. This is what survival is all about.

Freeing the Dying Heart

Highly sensitive, feeling people are an endangered species. Their hearts are hiding, dying. Their lives are wounded. They are being forced into chemical dependence and mechanization. They retreat from a high degree of sensitivity (sensitivity to the stress, hassle and pain of modern life) to save themselves. They risk killing off their souls. Without contact, without inspiration, life can be very difficult. Some of us break down. Some of us get sick. Some of us die. And some just live the limbo of soul-death, the most false and unhealthy death of all.

The pattern-addicted individual has made little and big decisions over a period of time to trade away the freedom of self-control in order to avoid and become numb to the challenges and pain of living. In so doing, pattern-addicted people are pressed to travel the path away from the heart. They have been compelled to live like machines. They have become creatures of habit, increasingly mechanical women and men. The life within their souls is draining away. A rock feels no pain, nor does a machine. It's that pain thing again. We work so hard to avoid the experience of pain that we do not see pain for what it is.

Ultimately, it is the experience of love that can free the addicted person and turn humanity away from the path of the robot. Seek the highest and purest path for your human heart. Love can transcend the intense lure of the land of no real feeling—the seemingly safe but very empty place of the dead heart. Something strange is happening to love. It is slipping away from us—all of us. Deciding to find love and to feel love again is the first step in freeing humanity's dying heart, the first step in life-healing. In this effort, we must all become like children taking our first steps, learning to explore the precious and fragile land of our truest feelings. In so doing, we preserve what is most human about us in an environment that pressures us to be more distant from our hearts, more machine-like, more automatic every day.

You can help us transcend the pressure to surrender free will. You can transcend. Yes, you can harvest each and every one of the deaths you undergo. Harvest the transcendence. Transcendence is life-healing. Navigating our hard times into higher states changes the meaning of these hard times. They become energy-full transitions, passages, initiations into new realms of ourselves and of the world around us. Each challenge is a doorway, an opening, a portal to an entire new energy matrix. Try it. Focus on letting go and stepping through to the new life you can have, the new life that is your birthright. Step through the portal, and transcend.

THE PORTAL

About the Author

Author, lecturer, psychotherapist and social scientist Dr. Angela deAngelis earned her two doctorates and two masters degrees at the University of California Berkeley, where she lectured in three departments for over a decade. Angela has served as a U.S. National Institute of Mental Health Postdoctoral Fellow; a U.S. Administration on Children, Youth and Families Fellow; and a U.S. Public Health Department Fellow. She has taught, researched, designed and implemented programs in several fields key to this work on the ongoing nature of the life force, among these being: loss and grief; adult, teen and child development; family violence; substance and behavioral addiction; and mental health. Over the past three decades, she has also worked directly in organizational, clinical, educational and faith settings, with several thousand persons experiencing emotional, substance, relationship and behavioral addictions and "co"-addictions, and other relationship challenges, as well as stress, anxiety and other "disorders." She has also worked with the children of many of the above. Dr. deAngelis is director of the Metaxis Institute based in Corte Madera, California.